Babcia Wera's Authentic Polish Cookbook

91 Easy Recipes to Enjoy the Rich, Comforting Flavors of Poland in Your Own Home & Share the Joy of Traditional Family Meals

Copyright © 2024 by HarvestGuard Publications - All rights reserved.

No portion of this book may be reproduced in any form without written permission from the publisher or author, except as permitted by U.S. copyright law.

This publication is designed to provide accurate and authoritative information in regard to the subject matter covered. It is sold with the understanding that neither the author nor the publisher is engaged in rendering legal, investment, accounting or other professional services. While the publisher and author have used their best efforts in preparing this book, they make no representations or warranties with respect to the accuracy or completeness of the contents of this book and specifically disclaim any implied warranties of merchantability or fitness for a particular purpose. No warranty may be created or extended by sales representatives or written sales materials. The advice and strategies contained herein may not be suitable for your situation. You should consult with a professional when appropriate. Neither the publisher nor the author shall be liable for any loss of profit or any other commercial damages, including but not limited to special, incidental, consequential, personal, or other damages.

Contents

Dedication	IV
Introduction	V
1. First Courses (Dania)	1
2. Soups (Zupy)	27
3. Appetizers (Przekąski)	43
4. Drinks (Napoje)	65
5. Desserts (Deserty)	77
Conclusion	99
6. Glossary	101
First Courses	
Soups	
Appetizers	
Drinks	
Desserts	

For my beloved children and grandchildren:

May these recipes bring you warmth, joy, and memories of home. May you always feel the love and tradition in each dish and carry our Polish heritage into the future with pride.

With all my heart, Babcia Wera.

Introduction

Nestled between Europe's majestic Carpathian Mountains and the amber shores of the Baltic Sea lies a land of rich history, vibrant culture, and unparalleled culinary delights. Welcome to Poland—a country where food is more than just sustenance; it is a celebration of heritage, a testament to resilience, and a reflection of the enduring spirit of its people.

In this cookbook, I invite you to embark on a journey through the culinary landscape of Poland—an experience that will tantalize your taste buds, awaken your senses, and transport you to the quaint kitchens and bustling markets of this remarkable nation. From hearty soups and stews to delicate pastries and desserts, each recipe is a window into the soul of Polish cuisine and into the soul of my family, offering a glimpse of our traditions, flavors, and stories that have shaped this culinary heritage for centuries.

At the heart of Polish cuisine lies a deep reverence for tradition. For generations, Polish families have passed down cherished recipes from grandmother to mother to daughter and from father to son, preserving the time-honored techniques and flavors that define this rich culinary tradition. Whether it's the comforting warmth of a bowl of żurek during Lent or the crispy perfection of a pierogi freshly made by loving hands, each dish carries with it a piece of Poland's cultural heritage and the heritage I grew up with—a connection to the past and a celebration of the present.

Yet, even as we celebrate tradition, we also embrace innovation. Polish cuisine is a dynamic fusion of influences from across Europe and beyond, reflecting centuries of trade, migration, and cultural exchange. From the hearty flavors of the highlander cuisine in the Tatra Mountains to the delicate pastries of the royal courts in Krakow. Poland's culinary landscape is as diverse as it is delicious. In the kitchens of Poland, ancient recipes mingle with modern ingredients, resulting in a vibrant tapestry of flavors that continues to evolve with each passing generation.

But perhaps what truly sets Polish cuisine apart is its emphasis on the communal aspect of dining. In Poland, food is meant to be shared, enjoyed, and celebrated with loved ones. Whether gathered around the table for a festive Wigilia supper or simply enjoying a cozy meal with family and friends, the act of eating is imbued with a sense of warmth and hospitality that is uniquely Polish. It is this spirit of togetherness that infuses every dish with a special magic—a magic that transforms a simple meal into a cherished memory.

As you journey through the pages of this cookbook, we hope you will not only discover new flavors and recipes but also gain a deeper appreciation for the cultural heritage that lies at the heart of Polish cuisine. From the earthy goodness of rustic farmhouse fare to the elegant refinement of noble banquet dishes, each recipe tells a story—a story of tradition, innovation, and the enduring bonds of family.

So grab your apron, sharpen your knives, and prepare to embark on a culinary adventure unlike any other. From the rustic charm of the countryside to the cosmopolitan bustle of the city streets, Poland awaits, ready to delight, inspire, and nourish both body and soul.

Zapraszamy was do Polski—Welcome to Poland. Welcome to a world of flavor, tradition, and togetherness. Welcome to the magic of Polish cuisine.

Chapter One
First Courses (Dania)

Pierogi (Polish Dumplings)

PREP TIME: 1 HOUR   COOKING TIME: 15 MIN   SERVES: 4-6 CALORIES PER SERVING: 300

Originally considered a peasant food, Pierogi were traditionally made by families in Poland as a way to use up any leftovers. Today, pierogi is a staple dish in Polish households and is a symbol of Polish culture and heritage.

Ingredients

You Need:
For the dough
- 2 cups all-purpose flour
- 1 large egg
- 1/2 cup sour cream
- 1/4 cup butter, softened
- 1/2 teaspoon salt

For the filling
- 2 cups mashed potatoes (cooled)
- 1 cup shredded cheddar cheese
- 1 small onion, finely chopped and sautéed until golden brown
- Salt and pepper to taste

Directions

- **Dough:** In a large mixing bowl, combine the flour and salt. Add the egg, sour cream, and softened butter to the flour mixture. Mix until a dough forms, then knead the dough on a lightly floured surface for about 5-7 minutes until smooth and elastic. Wrap the dough in plastic wrap and let it rest at room temperature for 30 minutes.

- **Filling:** In a separate bowl, mix together the mashed potatoes, shredded cheddar cheese, and sautéed onions. Season the filling with salt and pepper to taste. Set aside.

- **Assembly:** Roll out the dough on a floured surface to about 1/8 inch thickness. Use a round cookie cutter or glass to cut out circles of dough approximately 3 inches in diameter. Place a small spoonful of the potato filling in the center of each dough circle. Fold the dough over the filling to create a half-moon shape, then pinch the edges tightly to seal. Repeat with the remaining dough and filling.

- **Cooking:** Bring a large pot of salted water to a boil. Add pierogis in batches and cook until they float to the top, about 3-5 minutes.

You can also:
- The toppings are all optional. You can enjoy them with a bit of chopped chives and sour cream without all the extras.

Gołąbki (Stuffed Cabbage Rolls)

PREP TIME: 45 MIN   COOKING TIME: 1 HOUR   SERVES: 4-6   CALORIES PER SERVING: 350

Gołąbki, meaning "little pigeons" in Polish, is a dish that has been enjoyed in Poland and other Eastern European countries for centuries. It is believed to have been influenced by Turkish, Russian, and Jewish cuisines. Gołąbki is often served during special occasions.

Ingredients

You Need:

For the cabbage rolls
- 1 large head of cabbage
- 1 cup uncooked rice
- 1 pound ground beef
- 1 small onion, finely chopped
- 2 cloves garlic, minced
- 1 egg
- 1 teaspoon salt
- 1/2 teaspoon black pepper
- 1/2 teaspoon paprika
- 1/4 teaspoon dried thyme, oregano, and parsley

For the tomato sauce
- 2 cups tomato sauce
- 1 tablespoon brown sugar
- 1 tablespoon lemon juice
- Salt and pepper to taste

Directions

- **Prepare:** Bring a large pot of salted water to a boil. Remove the core from the cabbage and place the whole head in the boiling water. Cook for about 5-7 minutes or until the outer leaves are tender and can be easily peeled off. Remove the cabbage from the water and let cool. Once cool enough to handle, carefully peel off the softened outer leaves and set them aside.

- **Filling:** In a large mixing bowl, combine the uncooked rice, ground beef, chopped onion, minced garlic, egg, salt, pepper, paprika, thyme, oregano, and parsley. Mix until well combined.

- **Assembly:** Take a cabbage leaf and place a spoonful of the filling mixture in the center. Fold the sides of the cabbage leaf over the filling, then roll it up tightly to form a cabbage roll. Repeat. In a separate bowl, mix together the tomato sauce ingredients.

- **Cooking:** Preheat your oven to 350°F (175°C). Pour a thin layer of the tomato sauce into the bottom of a large baking dish. Arrange the cabbage rolls seam-side down in the baking dish. Pour the remaining tomato sauce over the cabbage rolls, covering them evenly. Cover the baking dish with foil and bake in the preheated oven for 45-50 minutes, or until the cabbage rolls are cooked through and the rice is tender.

Kotlet Schabowy (Breaded Pork Cutlet)

PREP TIME: 15 MIN **COOKING TIME: 15 MIN** **SERVES: 4** **CALORIES PER SERVING: 350**

Kotlet Schabowy is a popular Polish dish that has its roots in Austrian cuisine. It is believed to have been introduced to Poland during the time of the Austrian Empire's rule over parts of Poland.

Ingredients

You Need:

- 4 boneless pork chops, about 1/2-inch thick
- Salt and pepper to taste
- 1/2 cup all-purpose flour
- 2 large eggs, beaten
- 1 cup breadcrumbs (preferably Panko breadcrumbs for extra crispiness)
- Vegetable oil for frying
- Lemon wedges for serving

Optional:

- Serve with mashed potatoes or steamed vegetables

Directions

- **Prepare:** Place the pork chops between two sheets of plastic wrap or parchment paper. Using a meat mallet or rolling pin, pound the pork chops until they are about 1/4-inch thick. Season both sides of the pork chops with salt and pepper.

- **Breading Station:** Place the flour, beaten eggs, and breadcrumbs in three separate shallow bowls. Season the flour with a little salt and pepper.

- **Bread the Pork Chops:** Dredge each pork chop in the seasoned flour, shaking off any excess. Dip the floured pork chop into the beaten eggs, coating it evenly. Press the egg-coated pork chop into the breadcrumbs, making sure to coat it thoroughly on both sides. Gently shake off any excess breadcrumbs.

- **Frying:** In a large skillet, heat enough vegetable oil to cover the bottom of the pan over medium-high heat. Once the oil is hot, carefully add the breaded pork chops to the skillet, making sure not to overcrowd the pan. You may need to fry the pork chops in batches. Cook the pork chops for about 3-4 minutes on each side or until they are golden brown and cooked through. The internal temperature should reach 145°F (63°C). Transfer the cooked pork chops to a paper towel-lined plate to drain any excess oil.

Kiełbasa z Kapustą (Sausage with Sauerkraut)

PREP TIME: 10 MIN   COOKING TIME: 30 MIN   SERVES: 4-6 CALORIES PER SERVING: 350

Kiełbasa z Kapustą, which translates to "sausage with sauerkraut" in Polish, is a classic dish that reflects the hearty and rustic flavors of Polish cuisine. Sauerkraut, fermented cabbage, has been a staple in Eastern European diets for centuries and is believed to have originated as a method of preserving cabbage during the winter months.

Ingredients

You Need:

- 1 pound Polish kielbasa sausage, sliced into bite-sized pieces
- 1 tablespoon vegetable oil
- 1 onion, thinly sliced
- 2 cloves garlic, minced
- 1 pound sauerkraut, drained and rinsed
- 1 teaspoon caraway seeds (optional)
- Salt and pepper to taste
- 1 cup chicken or vegetable broth
- 1 tablespoon brown sugar (optional)
- Chopped fresh parsley for garnish (optional)

Directions

- **Prepare:** Heat the vegetable oil in a large skillet over medium heat. Add the sliced kielbasa sausage to the skillet and cook until browned on all sides, about 5-7 minutes. Remove the sausage from the skillet and set aside. In the same skillet, add the thinly sliced onion and minced garlic. Cook until the onions are soft and translucent, about 3-4 minutes. Add the sauerkraut to the skillet, along with the caraway seeds (if using), salt, and pepper. Stir to combine. Pour the chicken or vegetable broth over the sauerkraut mixture. Stir in the brown sugar if using.

- **Simmer the Dish:** Return the cooked sausage to the skillet and bring the mixture to a simmer. Reduce the heat to low, cover, and let it simmer for 20-25 minutes, stirring occasionally, until the flavors are well combined and the sauerkraut is tender.

You can also:

- Serve the dish with hot, crusty bread, boiled potatoes, or mashed potatoes.

Kopytka (Potato Dumplings)

PREP TIME: 20 MIN   COOKING TIME: 10 MIN   SERVES: 4   CALORIES PER SERVING: 250

Kopytka, which translates to "little hooves" in Polish, earned its name due to its shape resembling small hooves. These potato dumplings are a traditional Polish comfort food that originated as a way to use up leftover mashed potatoes.

Ingredients

You Need:

- 2 cups mashed potatoes (cooled)
- 1 egg
- 1 cup all-purpose flour, plus more for dusting
- Salt and pepper to taste
- 2 tablespoons butter
- Optional toppings: sautéed onions, crispy bacon bits, grated cheese, sour cream, chopped herbs

You can also:

- For added flavor, you can sauté the cooked dumplings in butter until they are golden brown and crispy on the outside.

Directions

- **Prepare:** If you don't have leftover mashed potatoes, boil peeled and diced potatoes until tender. Drain well and mash until smooth. Let the mashed potatoes cool completely before using in this recipe.

- **Prepare the Dough:** In a large mixing bowl, combine the cooled mashed potatoes with the egg, flour, salt, and pepper. Mix until a dough forms. If the dough is too sticky, add more flour, a tablespoon at a time, until it becomes manageable.

- **Shape the Dumplings:** Dust a clean work surface with flour. Take a portion of the dough and roll it into a rope about 1/2 inch thick. Cut the rope into 1-inch pieces. Using your hands, roll each piece into a small ball, then flatten it slightly to form a dumpling. Repeat with the remaining dough.

- **Boil the Dumplings:** Bring a large pot of salted water to a boil. Carefully drop the dumplings into the boiling water, working in batches if necessary to avoid overcrowding the pot. Cook the dumplings for about 3-4 minutes or until they float to the surface and are cooked through.

Placki Ziemniaczane (Potato Pancakes)

PREP TIME: 20 MIN   **COOKING TIME: 20 MIN**   **SERVES: 4**   **CALORIES PER SERVING: 250**

Placki Ziemniaczane, also known as Polish potato pancakes or latkes, are a beloved dish in Polish cuisine. They are often enjoyed as a savory snack or side dish, especially during the winter months and on special occasions like Hanukkah.

Ingredients

You Need:

- 4 medium russet potatoes, peeled
- 1 small onion, peeled
- 1 large egg
- 2 tablespoons all-purpose flour
- 1 teaspoon salt
- 1/2 teaspoon black pepper
- Vegetable oil for frying
- Sour cream, applesauce, or sugar for serving (optional)

You can also:

- Serve the Placki Ziemniaczane hot, with sour cream, applesauce, or a sprinkle of sugar on top if desired.

Directions

- **Prepare:** Using a box grater or a food processor fitted with a grating attachment, grate the peeled potatoes and onion. Place the grated mixture in a clean kitchen towel or cheesecloth and squeeze out as much liquid as possible.

- **Prepare the Batter:** In a large mixing bowl, combine the grated potatoes and onion with the egg, flour, salt, and black pepper. Mix until well combined.

- **Fry the Pancakes:** In a large skillet, heat enough vegetable oil over medium-high heat to cover the bottom of the pan. Once the oil is hot, drop spoonfuls of the potato mixture into the skillet, flattening them slightly with the back of the spoon. Cook the pancakes in batches, being careful not to overcrowd the pan. Fry the pancakes for 3-4 minutes on each side or until they are golden brown and crispy.

- **Drain and Serve:** Transfer the cooked potato pancakes to a paper towel-lined plate to drain any excess oil. Keep the pancakes warm in a low oven while you fry the remaining batches.

Śledź w Śmietanie (Herring in Cream Sauce)

PREP TIME: 20 MIN **COOKING TIME: 0 MIN** **SERVES: 4** **CALORIES PER SERVING: 250**

Śledź w Śmietanie, or marinated herring in cream sauce, is a classic Polish dish that is often enjoyed during festive occasions. Herring has been a staple in Polish cuisine for centuries, and this dish showcases the rich and savory flavors of marinated fish combined with creamy sauce.

Ingredients

You Need:

- 4 fillets of pickled herring, drained
- 1 small onion, thinly sliced
- 1/2 cup sour cream
- 2 tablespoons mayonnaise
- 1 tablespoon white wine vinegar or lemon juice
- 1 tablespoon granulated sugar
- Salt and pepper to taste
- Chopped fresh dill or parsley for garnish (optional)

Directions

- **Prepare:** Rinse the pickled herring fillets under cold water to remove excess brine. Pat them dry with paper towels and cut them into bite-sized pieces. Place the herring pieces in a shallow dish or container. In a small bowl, whisk together the sour cream, mayonnaise, white wine vinegar or lemon juice, and granulated sugar until smooth and well combined. Season with salt and pepper to taste.

- **Marinate the Herring:** Pour the marinade over the herring pieces, making sure they are evenly coated. Add the thinly sliced onion to the dish, distributing it evenly among the herring pieces. Cover the dish with plastic wrap and refrigerate for at least 4 hours or overnight to allow the flavors to meld.

- **Serve:** Once the herring has marinated, remove it from the refrigerator and let it come to room temperature for about 10-15 minutes before serving.

You can also:

- It's best served cold, but you can also serve it hot if you like. Sprinkle with fresh dill or parsley.

Zrazy (Beef Roulades)

PREP TIME: 30 MIN   COOKING TIME: 2 HOURS SERVES: 4-6 CALORIES PER SERVING: 400

The word "Zrazy" comes from the Polish verb "zrazic," which means to sear or brown meat. These tender beef rolls are typically stuffed with a savory filling and simmered until tender, resulting in a dish that's perfect for special occasions or family gatherings.

Ingredients

You Need:

- 1 1/2 pounds beef round or flank steak, thinly sliced into 4-6 pieces
- Salt and pepper to taste
- Dijon mustard or horseradish
- 1 onion, finely chopped
- 2 cloves garlic, minced
- 4 slices bacon, chopped
- 1/2 cup gherkins, finely chopped
- 2 tablespoons mustard
- 2 tablespoons tomato paste
- 1 cup beef broth
- 1 bay leaf
- 1 teaspoon dried thyme
- 1 teaspoon paprika
- 2 tablespoons oil
- Chopped fresh parsley for garnish (optional)

Directions

- **Prepare:** Season the thinly sliced beef pieces with salt and pepper on both sides. If desired, spread a thin layer of Dijon mustard or horseradish on one side of each beef slice. In a skillet, heat the vegetable oil over medium heat. Add the chopped onion, minced garlic, and chopped bacon. Cook until the onions are soft, and the bacon is crispy about 5-7 minutes. Stir in the chopped pickles, mustard, and tomato paste. Cook for another 2-3 minutes, then remove from heat and let cool slightly.

- **Assemble the Roulades:** Place a spoonful of the filling mixture on one end of each beef slice. Roll up the beef tightly, tucking in the sides as you go, to form a roulade. Secure each roulade with toothpicks or kitchen twine.

- **Spear the Roulades:** Once the roulades are browned, add the beef broth, bay leaf, dried thyme, and paprika to the skillet or Dutch oven. Bring the liquid to a simmer, then reduce the heat to low. Cover and simmer the roulades for about 1 1/2 to 2 hours, or until the beef is tender and cooked through and the flavors have melded together. Once the roulades are cooked, remove them from the skillet or Dutch oven and transfer them to a serving platter. Remove the toothpicks or kitchen twine.

Pierś z Kurczaka (Chicken Breast)

PREP TIME: 10 MIN   **COOKING TIME: 20 MINS**   **SERVES: 4**   **CALORIES PER SERVING: 250**

Pierś z Kurczaka, or chicken breast, is a versatile and popular ingredient in Polish cuisine, used in various dishes ranging from soups and stews to grilled or baked entrees. Chicken is widely enjoyed in Poland and is often featured in everyday meals as well as festive occasions.

Ingredients

You Need:

- 4 boneless, skinless chicken breast halves
- Salt and pepper to taste
- 2 tablespoons olive oil or melted butter
- Optional seasonings: garlic powder, paprika, dried herbs (such as thyme, rosemary, or oregano)

Directions

- **Preheat the Oven:** Preheat your oven to 375°F (190°C) if baking the chicken breast.

- **Prepare the Chicken:** Season both sides of the chicken breast halves with salt, pepper, and any optional seasonings of your choice, such as garlic powder, paprika, or dried herbs. Rub the seasonings into the chicken to ensure even flavoring.

- **Bake the Chicken:** Place the seasoned chicken breast halves in a single layer in a baking dish. Drizzle with olive oil or melted butter, or brush the tops with a little oil or butter. Bake in the preheated oven for 18-20 minutes or until the chicken is cooked through and no longer pink in the center. The internal temperature should reach 165°F (75°C). Remove the chicken from the oven and let it rest for a few minutes before serving.

You can also:

- Serve your chicken breast on a bed of mashed potatoes and a side of green beans or vegetable of your choice.

Kaszanka (Polish Blood Sausage)

PREP TIME: 20 MIN   **COOKING TIME: 30 MIN**   **SERVES: 4-6   CALORIES PER SERVING: 250**

Kaszanka, also known as "kiszka" or "krupniok" in some regions of Poland, is a traditional Polish blood sausage that has been enjoyed for centuries. It is typically made with a mixture of pork meat, pork blood, and buckwheat or barley groats, seasoned with onions, garlic, and spices.

Ingredients

You Need:
- 1 pound pork blood (available at specialty butcher shops or online)
- 1/2 pound pork liver, finely chopped
- 1/2 pound pork fatback or bacon, finely chopped
- 1 cup cooked buckwheat or barley groats (kasha), cooled
- 1 onion, finely chopped
- 2 cloves garlic, minced
- 1 teaspoon salt
- 1/2 teaspoon black pepper
- 1/2 teaspoon marjoram
- 1/4 teaspoon allspice
- Natural sausage casings or synthetic casings (available at specialty stores)

Directions

- **Prepare the Casings** If using natural sausage casings, rinse them thoroughly under cold water to remove any salt or debris. Soak the casings in warm water for about 30 minutes to soften them before using. If using synthetic casings, follow the manufacturer's instructions for preparation.

- **Mix the Ingredients:** In a large mixing bowl, combine the pork blood, finely chopped pork liver, pork fatback or bacon, cooked buckwheat or barley groats, chopped onion, minced garlic, salt, pepper, marjoram, and allspice. Mix until all the ingredients are well combined.

- **Stuff the Casings:** Using a sausage stuffer or a funnel, fill the prepared sausage casings with the mixture, leaving a little space at the ends to tie them off. Twist the casings at regular intervals to form individual sausage links.

- **Cook the Sausage:** Bring a large pot of water to a gentle simmer. Carefully add the stuffed sausage casings to the pot, making sure they are fully submerged. Simmer the kaszanka for about 20-30 minutes or until they are fully cooked through. Once cooked, remove the kaszanka from the pot and let them cool slightly.

Flaki (Tripe Stew)

PREP TIME: 30 MIN   COOKING TIME: 2 HOURS SERVES: 4-6 CALORIES PER SERVING: 350

Flaki, also known as "flaczki" in Polish, is a traditional Polish dish that has been enjoyed for centuries. It is a hearty stew made with beef tripe, vegetables, and spices, and is often served as a comforting and nourishing meal, especially during the colder months.

Ingredients

You Need:

- 1 pound beef tripe, cleaned and cut into small pieces
- 1 onion, finely chopped
- 2 carrots, peeled and diced
- 2 celery stalks, diced
- 2 cloves garlic, minced
- 1 bay leaf
- 1 teaspoon dried marjoram
- Salt and pepper to taste
- 8 cups beef broth or water
- 2 tablespoons tomato paste
- 2 tablespoons all-purpose flour
- 2 tablespoons unsalted butter

Directions

- **Prepare the Tripe:** Rinse the beef tripe under cold water and remove any excess fat or membrane. Cut the tripe into small, bite-sized pieces and set aside.

- **Cook the Tripe:** In a large pot, bring the beef broth or water to a boil over medium-high heat. Add the tripe pieces to the pot and cook for about 30 minutes, skimming off any foam or impurities that rise to the surface. After 30 minutes, add the chopped onion, diced carrots, diced celery, minced garlic, bay leaf, dried marjoram, salt, and pepper to the pot. Stir to combine and reduce the heat to low. Cover the pot and let the stew simmer gently for about 1 1/2 hours or until the tripe is tender and the vegetables are cooked through.

- **Thicken the Stew:** In a small bowl, mix together the tomato paste and flour until smooth. Stir in a ladleful of hot broth from the pot to temper the mixture. Gradually add the tomato paste mixture back to the pot, stirring constantly, to thicken the stew. Simmer for an additional 10-15 minutes, uncovered, to allow the flavors to meld and the stew to thicken slightly. Once the stew is ready, remove the bay leaf from the pot. Taste and adjust the seasoning if necessary. Stir in the unsalted butter until melted and well incorporated. Ladle the hot flaki into bowls.

Kluski Śląskie (Silesian Dumplings)

PREP TIME: 15 MIN   **COOKING TIME: 25 MIN**   **SERVES: 4**   **CALORIES PER SERVING: 300**

Kotlety Mielone, or Polish meatballs, are a classic comfort food in Polish cuisine. These meatballs are known for their savory flavor and tender texture, making them a favorite among both children and adults.

Ingredients

You Need:

- 4 medium potatoes, peeled and cut into chunks
- 1 cup potato starch
- 1 egg
- Salt to taste
- Optional: chopped fresh parsley or chives for garnish

Directions

- **Prepare the Potatoes:** Place the peeled and chopped potatoes in a large pot of salted water. Bring to a boil over medium-high heat, then reduce the heat to medium-low and simmer until the potatoes are tender about 15-20 minutes. Drain the cooked potatoes and transfer them to a large mixing bowl. Mash the potatoes until smooth and free of lumps. Allow the mashed potatoes to cool slightly. Once the mashed potatoes have cooled slightly, add the potato starch and egg to the bowl. Mix until well combined and a dough begins to form. The dough should be soft and slightly sticky.

- **Shape the Dumplings:** Divide the dough into equal portions and shape each portion into a small oval-shaped dumpling, about 2 inches in length.cUse a spoon or your hands to shape the dumplings, and lightly coat them with potato starch to prevent sticking.

- **Cook the Dumplings:** Bring a large pot of salted water to a gentle boil. Carefully drop the dumplings into the boiling water, working in batches if necessary to avoid overcrowding the pot. Cook the dumplings for about 5-7 minutes or until they float to the surface and are cooked through.

Kotlety Mielone (Polish Meatballs)

PREP TIME: 15 MIN   **COOKING TIME: 25 MIN**   **SERVES: 4**   **CALORIES PER SERVING: 300**

Kotlety Mielone, or Polish meatballs, are a classic comfort food in Polish cuisine. These meatballs are known for their savory flavor and tender texture, making them a favorite among both children and adults.

Ingredients

You Need:

- 1 pound ground beef (or a mixture of beef and pork)
- 1 small onion, finely chopped
- 1 clove garlic, minced
- 1/2 cup breadcrumbs
- 1 egg
- 2 tablespoons milk
- 1 teaspoon Worcestershire sauce (optional)
- 1 teaspoon Dijon mustard (optional)
- 1 teaspoon dried oregano
- 1/2 teaspoon paprika
- Salt and pepper to taste
- 2 tablespoons vegetable oil for frying

Directions

- **Prepare the Meat Mixture:** In a large mixing bowl, combine the ground beef, finely chopped onion, minced garlic, breadcrumbs, egg, milk, Worcestershire sauce (if using), Dijon mustard (if using), dried oregano, paprika, salt, and pepper. Mix until all the ingredients are well combined.

- **Shape the Meatballs:** Using your hands, shape the meat mixture into golf ball-sized meatballs. Roll each meatball between your palms to ensure they are evenly shaped.

- **Cook the Meatballs:** Heat the vegetable oil in a large skillet over medium heat. Once the oil is hot, add the meatballs to the skillet in a single layer, making sure not to overcrowd the pan. You may need to cook the meatballs in batches, depending on the size of your skillet. Cook the meatballs for about 4-5 minutes on each side or until they are browned and cooked through. You can check for doneness by cutting into one of the meatballs to ensure there is no pinkness in the center.

Żurek (Sour Rye Soup)

PREP TIME: 15 MIN   **COOKING TIME: 1 HR 30**   **SERVES: 6**   **CALORIES PER SERVING: 300**

Żurek is a traditional Polish soup that has been enjoyed for centuries, especially during Easter celebrations. It is known for its distinctive sour flavor, which comes from the fermentation of rye flour or sourdough bread.

Ingredients

You Need:
- 6 cups chicken or vegetable broth
- 1 cup dried forest mushrooms
- 1 cup sourdough bread or rye flour
- 1 onion, finely chopped
- 2 cloves garlic, minced
- 1 tablespoon vegetable oil
- 1/2 pound Polish sausage, sliced
- 2 medium potatoes, peeled and diced
- 1 cup sour cream
- 2 tablespoons all-purpose flour
- 2 bay leaves
- 1 teaspoon dried marjoram
- Salt and pepper to taste
- Hard-boiled eggs and chopped fresh parsley for serving (optional)

Directions

- **Prepare the Broth:** In a large pot, bring the chicken or vegetable broth to a simmer over medium heat. If using dried mushrooms, strain the soaking liquid through a fine-mesh sieve lined with cheesecloth or a paper towel to remove any grit, and add the liquid to the pot. Discard the soaked mushrooms.
- **Prepare the Sour Dough Starter:** Ladle some of the hot broth over the shredded bread pieces and let them soak for about 10 minutes until softened.
- **Saute:** In a skillet, heat the vegetable oil over medium heat. Add the chopped onion and minced garlic and sauté until softened and fragrant, about 5 minutes. Add the sliced Polish sausage and diced potatoes to the pot with the simmering broth. Stir in the sautéed onion and garlic mixture, along with the bay leaves and dried marjoram. Season with salt and pepper to taste.
- **Simmer and Thicken the Soup:** Let the soup simmer over low heat for about 1 hour, stirring occasionally, until the potatoes are tender and the flavors have melded together. Whisk together sour cream and flour until smooth. Gradually add a ladleful of hot broth from the pot to the sour cream mixture, stirring constantly, to temper it. Add the tempered sour cream mixture back to the pot, stirring constantly, to thicken the soup. Simmer for an additional 10-15 minutes, uncovered, to allow the flavors to meld and the soup to thicken slightly.

Kluski z Makiem (Poppy Seed Noodles)

PREP TIME: 30 MIN   COOKING TIME: 10 MIN   SERVES: 4   CALORIES PER SERVING: 350

Kluski z Makiem, or Poppy Seed Noodles, is a traditional Polish dish often served during Christmas Eve supper (Wigilia). It's a dish that combines tender noodles with a sweet and nutty poppy seed filling, creating a delightful dessert or treat for special occasions.

Ingredients

You Need:

For the noodles
- 8 ounces wide egg noodles
- Water for boiling
- Pinch of salt

For the poppy seed filling
- 1 cup ground poppy seeds
- 1/2 cup honey or sugar
- 1/4 cup milk
- 2 tablespoons unsalted butter
- 1/2 teaspoon vanilla extract
- Zest of 1 lemon
- Pinch of ground cinnamon
- Pinch of salt

For garnish (optional)
- Powdered sugar
- Chopped nuts (such as walnuts or almonds)

Directions

- **Cook the Noodles:** Bring a large pot of salted water to a boil. Add the egg noodles and cook according to package instructions until al dente. Drain the noodles and set aside.

- **Prepare the Poppy Seed Filling:** In a saucepan, combine the ground poppy seeds, honey or sugar, milk, unsalted butter, vanilla extract, lemon zest, ground cinnamon, and a pinch of salt. Cook over medium heat, stirring constantly, until the mixture thickens slightly and becomes fragrant about 5-7 minutes. Remove from heat and let the filling cool slightly.

- **Combine:** Transfer the cooked egg noodles to a large mixing bowl. Pour the warm poppy seed filling over the noodles and toss gently until the noodles are evenly coated with the filling.

Golonka (Pork Knuckle)

PREP TIME: 15 MIN   COOKING TIME: 3 HOURS   SERVES: 4-6 CALORIES PER SERVING: 500

Golonka, or Pork Knuckle, is a popular dish in Polish cuisine, especially enjoyed during festive occasions and gatherings. It is known for its tender, succulent meat and crispy skin, making it a hearty and satisfying meal.

Ingredients

You Need:
- 1 pork knuckle (approximately 3-4 pounds)
- 1 onion, peeled and quartered
- 2 carrots, peeled and roughly chopped
- 2 celery stalks, roughly chopped
- 4 garlic cloves, peeled and smashed
- 2 bay leaves
- 1 tablespoon black peppercorns
- 1 tablespoon whole allspice berries
- 1 tablespoon caraway seeds
- 2 tablespoons salt
- Water, enough to cover the pork knuckle

Directions

- **Prepare the Pork Knuckle:** Place the pork knuckle in a large container or resealable plastic bag. Add the quartered onion, chopped carrots, chopped celery, smashed garlic cloves, bay leaves, black peppercorns, allspice berries, caraway seeds, and salt. Pour enough water over the pork knuckle to completely submerge it in the marinade. Seal the container or bag and refrigerate overnight, or for at least 12 hours, to allow the flavors to infuse.

- **Cook the Pork Knuckle:** Preheat your oven to 325°F (160°C). Remove the pork knuckle from the marinade and discard the marinade and aromatics. Pat the pork knuckles dry with paper towels. Place the pork knuckle on a rack set inside a roasting pan or baking dish. Roast the pork knuckle in the preheated oven for 3 hours, or until the meat is tender and the skin is crispy and golden brown.

- **Rest:** Once the pork knuckle is cooked through, remove it from the oven and let it rest for 10-15 minutes before carving.

Krokiety (Croquettes)

PREP TIME: 30 MIN   COOKING TIME: 20 MIN   SERVES: 12-15   CALORIES PER SERVING: 350

Krokiety, or Croquettes, are a popular Polish dish enjoyed as a savory snack or appetizer. They are made by rolling a filling of cooked meat, vegetables, and cheese in thin crepes, then coating them in breadcrumbs and frying until crispy.

Ingredients

You Need:

For the crepes
- 1 cup all-purpose flour
- 2 large eggs
- 1 cup milk
- Pinch of salt
- Butter or oil for frying

For the filling
- 1 cup cooked chicken or ham
- 1 small onion, finely chopped
- 1 carrot, grated
- 1/2 cup mushrooms, finely chopped
- 1/2 cup grated cheese
- Salt and pepper to taste
- 2 tablespoons butter
- 2 tablespoons all-purpose flour
- 1 cup milk
- 1/2 cup broth
- 1/2 teaspoon dried thyme or parsley
- Breadcrumbs for coating
- Oil for frying

Directions

- **Make the Crepes:** Whisk flour, eggs, milk, and salt in a bowl until smooth. Heat a small non-stick skillet over medium heat and lightly grease with butter or oil. Pour a small amount of batter into the skillet, swirling to coat the bottom evenly. Cook each crepe for 1-2 minutes per side until golden brown. Repeat. Stack on a plate and set aside.
- **Prepare the Filling:** Melt butter in a large skillet over medium heat. Add chopped onion, grated carrot, and chopped mushrooms. Cook for about 5 minutes until softened. Stir in cooked chicken or ham. Season with salt and pepper. Remove from heat and set aside.
- **Make the Sauce:** Melt butter in a small saucepan over medium heat. Stir in flour to form a paste. Gradually whisk in milk and chicken or vegetable broth until smooth. Cook, stirring constantly, until thickened. Add dried thyme or parsley, and season with salt and pepper. Let cool slightly.
- **Assemble and Fry:** Place a spoonful of the filling onto each crepe and roll up tightly, tucking in the sides. Arrange seam-side down in a baking dish. Heat oil in a deep frying pan or skillet over medium-high heat. Dip each rolled crepe in the sauce, then coat evenly in breadcrumbs. Fry the coated croquettes until golden brown and crispy, about 2-3 minutes per side. Drain on paper towels.

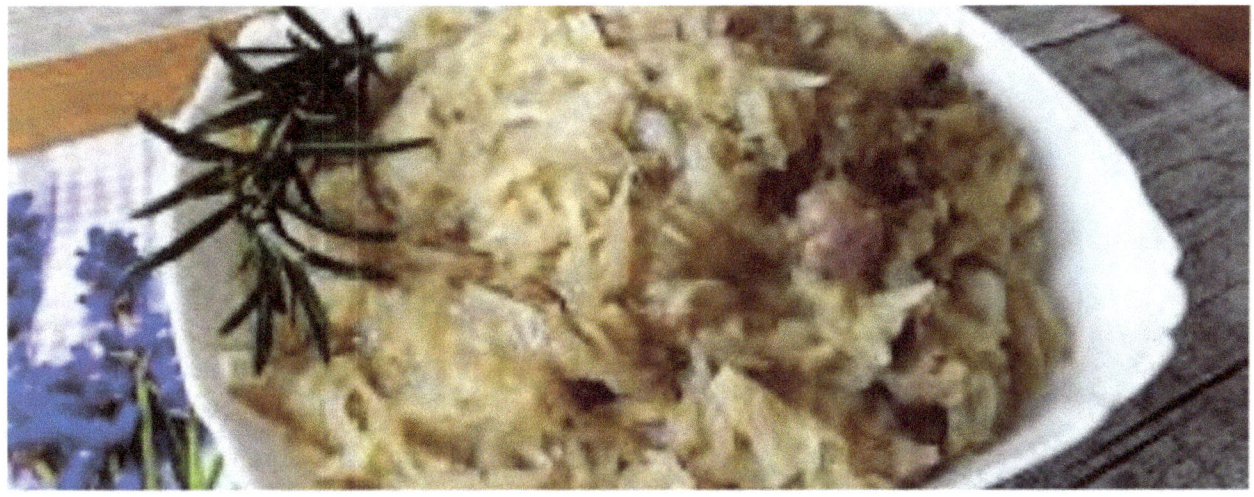

Kapusta Zasmażana (Caramelized Cabbage)

PREP TIME: 10 MIN   COOKING TIME: 30 MIN   SERVES: 4-6   CALORIES PER SERVING: 150

Kapusta Zasmażana, or Caramelized Cabbage, is a traditional Polish dish that transforms humble cabbage into a flavorful and comforting side dish. Caramelizing the cabbage brings out its natural sweetness, while the addition of onions and seasonings adds depth of flavor.

Ingredients

You Need:

- 1 medium head of cabbage, thinly sliced
- 1 large onion, thinly sliced
- 2 tablespoons butter or vegetable oil
- 1 tablespoon granulated sugar
- 1 teaspoon salt
- 1/2 teaspoon black pepper
- 1/2 teaspoon caraway seeds (optional)
- Chopped fresh parsley for garnish (optional)

You can also:

- Garnish with parsley.

Directions

- **Prepare:** Rinse the cabbage under cold water and remove any tough outer leaves. Cut the cabbage in half, then thinly slice each half into shreds. Peel and thinly slice the onion.

- **Caramelize:** In a large skillet or frying pan, melt the butter or heat the vegetable oil over medium heat. Add the sliced onion to the skillet and cook, stirring occasionally, until softened and translucent, about 5 minutes. Add the sliced cabbage to the skillet and toss to combine with the onions.

- **Cook:** Cook the cabbage and onions, stirring occasionally, until the cabbage starts to wilt and release its juices, about 10-15 minutes. Sprinkle the granulated sugar, salt, black pepper, and caraway seeds (if using) over the cabbage mixture. Stir well to combine, ensuring that the seasonings are evenly distributed. Cook the cabbage mixture, stirring occasionally, until the cabbage is tender and caramelized and most of the liquid has evaporated, about 15-20 minutes more. Adjust the seasoning to taste, if necessary.

Kopytka ze Śmietaną (Potato Dumplings with Sour Cream)

PREP TIME: 30 MIN   COOKING TIME: 15 MIN   SERVES: 4-6   CALORIES PER SERVING: 300

Kopytka ze Śmietaną, or Potato Dumplings with Sour Cream, is a classic Polish comfort food that is simple to make and incredibly satisfying. These dumplings are made from mashed potatoes, flour, and egg, and are served with a generous dollop of sour cream for a creamy and flavorful dish.

Ingredients

You Need:

For the potato dumplings
- 2 large potatoes, peeled and cut into chunks
- 1 egg
- 1 cup all-purpose flour, plus more for dusting
- Salt to taste
- Water for boiling

For serving
- Sour cream
- Chopped fresh parsley or chives (optional)

You can also:
- Garnish with sour cream.

Directions

- **Cook and mash the Potatoes:** Place the peeled and chopped potatoes in a large pot of salted water. Bring to a boil over medium-high heat, then reduce the heat to medium-low and simmer until the potatoes are tender about 15-20 minutes. Drain the cooked potatoes and transfer them to a large mixing bowl. Mash the cooked potatoes using a potato masher or fork until smooth and free of lumps.
- **Make the Dough:** Add the egg and flour to the mashed potatoes. Season with salt to taste. Mix until all the ingredients are well combined and a dough forms. The dough should be soft and slightly sticky.
- **Shape the Dumplings:** Dust a clean work surface with flour. Take a small portion of the dough and roll it into a rope about 1/2 inch in diameter. Cut the rope into small pieces, about 1 inch long. Use your hands to shape each piece into a small dumpling, pressing lightly to flatten the top.
- **Boil the Dumplings:** Bring a large pot of salted water to a gentle boil. Carefully drop the dumplings into the boiling water. Cook the dumplings for about 3-5 minutes or until they float to the surface and are cooked through. Use a slotted spoon to remove the cooked dumplings from the water and transfer them to a serving dish.

Kapusta Zasmażana z Kiełbasą (Caramelized Cabbage with Sausage)

PREP TIME: 15 MIN   COOKING TIME: 45 MIN   SERVES: 4-6   CALORIES PER SERVING: 350

Kapusta Zasmażana z Kiełbasą, or Caramelized Cabbage with Sausage, is a hearty and flavorful Polish dish that combines the sweet and savory flavors of caramelized cabbage with the smoky richness of sausage.

Ingredients

You Need:
- 1 medium head of cabbage, thinly sliced
- 1 large onion, thinly sliced
- 2 tablespoons butter or vegetable oil
- 1 tablespoon granulated sugar
- 1 teaspoon salt
- 1/2 teaspoon black pepper
- 1/2 teaspoon caraway seeds (optional)
- 1 pound Polish sausage (kielbasa), sliced into rounds
- Chopped fresh parsley for garnish (optional)

You can also:
- Garnish with freshly chopped parsley.

Directions

- **Prepare:** Rinse the cabbage under cold water and remove any tough outer leaves. Cut the cabbage in half, then thinly slice each half into shreds. Peel and thinly slice the onion.

- **Caramelize:** In a large skillet or frying pan, melt the butter or heat the vegetable oil over medium heat. Add the sliced onion to the skillet and cook, stirring occasionally, until softened and translucent, about 5 minutes. Add the sliced cabbage to the skillet and toss to combine with the onions.

- **Cook:** Cook the cabbage and onions, stirring occasionally, until the cabbage starts to wilt and release its juices, about 10-15 minutes. Sprinkle the granulated sugar, salt, black pepper, and caraway seeds (if using) over the cabbage mixture. Stir well to combine, ensuring that the seasonings are evenly distributed.

- **Add Sausage:** Add the sliced Polish sausage to the skillet with the cabbage mixture. Continue to cook, stirring occasionally, until the sausage is heated through and the cabbage is caramelized and tender, about 15-20 minutes more.

Krokiety z Mięsem (Meat Croquettes)

PREP TIME: 30 MIN   COOKING TIME: 20 MIN   SERVES: 12-15   CALORIES PER SERVING: 200

Krokiety z Mięsem, or Meat Croquettes, are a popular Polish dish that combines savory meat filling with a crispy breadcrumb coating.

Ingredients

You Need:

For the meat filling
- 1 pound ground beef or pork
- 1 onion, finely chopped
- 2 cloves garlic, minced
- 1 carrot, grated
- 1/2 cup breadcrumbs
- 1/4 cup milk
- 1 teaspoon dried thyme or parsley
- Salt and pepper to taste
- 2 tablespoons vegetable oil for frying

For the croquette coating
- 2 eggs, beaten
- 1 cup breadcrumbs
- Oil for frying

Directions

- **Prepare:** In a skillet, heat the vegetable oil over medium heat. Add the chopped onion and minced garlic, and sauté until softened and fragrant, about 5 minutes. Add the ground beef or pork to the skillet and cook until browned. Stir in the grated carrot, breadcrumbs, milk, dried thyme or parsley, salt, and pepper. Cook for 5 minutes. Remove from heat and let the filling cool slightly.

- **Shape:** Take a spoonful of the meat filling and shape it into a small cylinder or oval shape, about 2-3 inches long. Make 12-15 croquettes.

- **Coat:** Dip each meat croquette into the beaten eggs, then roll it in the breadcrumbs until evenly coated. Place the coated croquettes on a plate or baking sheet lined with parchment paper.

- **Fry:** In a large skillet or frying pan, heat enough oil to cover the bottom of the pan over medium-high heat. Once the oil is hot, carefully add the coated croquettes to the pan in batches, making sure not to overcrowd the pan. Fry the croquettes for about 3-4 minutes on each side or until golden brown and crispy. Use a slotted spoon to transfer the fried croquettes to a plate lined with paper towels to drain excess oil.

Zupa Pomidorowa (Tomato Soup)

PREP TIME: 15 MIN   COOKING TIME: 30 MIN   SERVES: 4-6   CALORIES PER SERVING: 200

Zupa Pomidorowa, or Tomato Soup, is a beloved classic in Polish cuisine, known for its rich and comforting flavor. It's a versatile dish that can be served hot or cold, making it perfect for any time of year.

Ingredients

You Need:

- 2 tablespoons butter or olive oil
- 1 onion, chopped
- 2 cloves garlic, minced
- 2 pounds ripe tomatoes, chopped (or 2 cans of diced tomatoes)
- 1 tablespoon tomato paste
- 4 cups vegetable or chicken broth
- 1 teaspoon sugar
- Salt and pepper to taste
- 1/2 cup heavy cream or sour cream (optional)
- Chopped fresh basil or parsley for garnish (optional)

Directions

- **Prepare:** Heat the butter or olive oil in a large pot over medium heat. Add the chopped onion and minced garlic, and sauté until softened and fragrant, about 5 minutes.

- **Add Tomatoes:** Add the chopped tomatoes and tomato paste to the pot and cook for another 5 minutes, stirring occasionally.

- **Simmer:** Pour in the vegetable or chicken broth and bring the soup to a simmer. Cover the pot and let the soup cook for about 20 minutes, allowing the flavors to meld together and the tomatoes to break down.

- **Season:** Stir in the sugar, salt, and pepper to taste. Adjust the seasoning as needed, depending on your preference for sweetness and saltiness.

- **Blend:** Once the soup is cooked, use an immersion blender to blend it until smooth. Alternatively, you can transfer the soup to a blender in batches and blend it until smooth. Be careful when blending hot liquids.

- **Add Cream:** If using heavy cream or sour cream, stir it into the blended soup until well combined.

Jajka w Sosie Tatarskim (Eggs in Tartar Sauce)

PREP TIME: 10 MIN   COOKING TIME: 15 MIN   SERVES: 4   CALORIES PER SERVING: 200

Jajka w Sosie Tatarskim, or Eggs in Tartar Sauce, is a traditional Polish dish that combines boiled eggs with a tangy and creamy tartar sauce.

Ingredients

You Need:
For the boiled eggs
- 8 eggs
- Water for boiling

For the tartar sauce
- 1/2 cup mayonnaise
- 2 tablespoons chopped pickles
- 1 tablespoon chopped capers
- 1 tablespoon chopped fresh parsley
- 1 teaspoon Dijon mustard
- 1 teaspoon lemon juice
- Salt and pepper to taste

For serving (optional)
- Chopped fresh chives or parsley for garnish
- Toasted bread or crackers

Directions

- **Boil Eggs:** Place the eggs in a large pot and cover them with cold water. Bring the water to a boil over high heat. Once boiling, reduce the heat to medium-low and let the eggs simmer for 10-12 minutes. Remove the pot from heat and immediately transfer the eggs to a bowl of ice water to cool completely. Once cooled, peel the eggs and set aside.

- **PrepareTartare Sauce:** In a small bowl, combine the mayonnaise, chopped pickles, chopped capers, chopped fresh parsley, Dijon mustard, lemon juice, salt, and pepper. Stir until all the ingredients are well combined and the sauce is smooth and creamy. Adjust the seasoning to taste, if necessary.

- **Assemble:** Slice the boiled eggs in half lengthwise and arrange them on a serving platter or individual plates. Spoon the tartar sauce generously over the eggs, covering them completely.

- **Garnish:** Sprinkle the chopped fresh chives or parsley over the eggs for a pop of color and added flavor.

Ryba po Grecku (Polish Greek-Style Fish)

PREP TIME: 15 MIN   COOKING TIME: 30 MIN   SERVES: 4-6   CALORIES PER SERVING: 300

Despite its name, Ryba po Grecku, or Polish Greek-Style Fish, is a traditional Polish dish with no direct connection to Greek cuisine. It's a flavorful and comforting dish made with fish fillets cooked in a tangy tomato sauce with onions, carrots, and spices.

Ingredients

You Need:

- 1.5 pounds white fish fillets (such as cod, haddock, or pollock)
- 2 tablespoons olive oil
- 1 onion, thinly sliced
- 2 carrots, grated
- 2 garlic cloves, minced
- 1 can (14 ounces) diced tomatoes
- 1 tablespoon tomato paste
- 1 teaspoon paprika
- 1/2 teaspoon dried oregano
- Salt and pepper to taste
- Fresh parsley or dill for garnish (optional)

Directions

- **Prepare the Fish:** Rinse the fish fillets under cold water and pat them dry with paper towels. Season the fish with salt and pepper on both sides.
- **Cook the Vegetables:** In a large skillet or frying pan, heat the olive oil over medium heat. Add the sliced onion and grated carrots to the skillet and cook, stirring occasionally, until softened, about 5 minutes. Add the minced garlic to the skillet and cook for an additional minute until fragrant.
- **Prepare the Sauce:** Stir in the diced tomatoes, tomato paste, paprika, dried oregano, salt, and pepper to the skillet with the cooked vegetables. Bring the sauce to a simmer and let it cook for about 10 minutes, allowing the flavors to meld together and the sauce to thicken slightly.
- **Cook Fish:** Once the tomato sauce is ready, gently place the seasoned fish fillets into the skillet, making sure they are submerged in the sauce. Cover the skillet and let the fish simmer in the sauce for about 10-15 minutes, or until the fish is cooked through and flakes easily with a fork.

You can also:

- Serve wit hot crusty bread or steamed white rice. Garnish with parsley before serving.

Kulebiak (Fish Pie)

PREP TIME: 30 MIN   COOKING TIME: 1 HOUR   SERVES: 6-8   CALORIES PER SERVING: 500

Kulebiak, also known as Coulibiac or Russian Fish Pie, is a traditional dish that originated in Russia but is also popular in Polish cuisine. It typically consists of flaky pastry dough filled with layers of fish, rice or potatoes, vegetables, and herbs, all baked to golden perfection.

Ingredients

You Need:

For the pastry dough
- 2 cups all-purpose flour
- 1/2 teaspoon salt
- 1/2 cup cold butter, cut into small cubes
- 1/2 cup cold water

For the filling
- 1 pound boneless, skinless fish fillets (such as salmon, trout, or cod)
- 1 cup cooked rice or mashed potatoes
- 1 onion, finely chopped
- 2 cloves garlic, minced
- 1 carrot, grated
- 1/2 cup frozen peas
- 2 hard-boiled eggs, chopped
- 2 tablespoons chopped fresh dill
- Salt and pepper to taste
- 1 egg, beaten (for egg wash)

Directions

- **Prepare the Pastry:** In a large mixing bowl, combine the flour and salt. Add the cold butter cubes and use a pastry cutter or fork to cut the butter into the flour until the mixture resembles coarse crumbs. Gradually add the cold water, mixing until the dough comes together. Shape the dough into a ball, wrap it in plastic wrap, and refrigerate for at least 30 minutes. Preheat your oven to 375°F (190°C).

- **Prepare the Filling:** In a skillet, heat a tablespoon of oil over medium heat. Add the chopped onion and minced garlic, and sauté until softened and fragrant, about 5 minutes. Add the grated carrot and frozen peas to the skillet and cook for an additional 2-3 minutes. Remove the skillet from heat and let the vegetable mixture cool slightly.

- **Assemble the Pie:** Roll out the chilled pastry dough on a lightly floured surface into a large rectangle about 1/4 inch thick. Place half of the rolled-out dough on the prepared baking sheet. Arrange the fish fillets on top of the dough, leaving a border around the edges. Season the fish with salt and pepper. Add filling. Fold the dough over the pie. Brush with beaten egg and bake for 45 to 50 minutes.

CHAPTER TWO
SOUPS (ZUPY)

Barszcz (Beet Soup)

PREP TIME: 15 MIN   COOKING TIME: 1 HOUR   SERVES: 4-6   CALORIES PER SERVING: 150

Barszcz, also known as Borscht, is a traditional Eastern European soup that has been enjoyed for centuries. It is particularly popular in Polish, Ukrainian, Russian, and Jewish cuisines.

Ingredients

You Need:

- 4 medium beets, peeled and grated
- 1 onion, finely chopped
- 2 cloves garlic, minced
- 4 cups vegetable or beef broth
- 2 tablespoons olive oil or butter
- 2 tablespoons red wine vinegar or lemon juice
- 1 tablespoon granulated sugar
- Salt and pepper to taste
- Sour cream and chopped fresh dill for serving (optional)

Directions

- **Prepare the Vegetables:** Peel the beets and grate them using a box grater or food processor. Finely chop the onion and mince the garlic. In a large pot, heat the olive oil or butter over medium heat. Add the chopped onion and minced garlic to the pot and sauté until softened and fragrant, about 5 minutes. Add the grated beets to the pot with the onions and garlic and stir to combine. Cook for another 5 minutes, allowing the beets to release their juices and soften slightly. Add the vegetable or beef broth to the pot with the beets, onions, and garlic. Bring the soup to a simmer over medium heat.

- **Season the Soup:** Stir in the red wine vinegar or lemon juice, granulated sugar, salt, and pepper to taste. Adjust the seasoning according to your taste preferences.

- **Simmer the Soup:** Reduce the heat to low and let the soup simmer, uncovered, for about 45 minutes to 1 hour, or until the beets are tender and the flavors have melded together.

You can also:

- Serve with a dollop of sour cream.

Żurek (Sour Rye Soup)

PREP TIME: 15 MIN   COOKING TIME: 1 HOUR   SERVES: 6-8   CALORIES PER SERVING: 250

Żurek is a traditional Polish soup that is often enjoyed during Easter celebrations, but it's also popular year-round. One unique ingredient in Żurek is "żur," which is a fermented rye flour mixture that gives the soup its characteristic sour flavor and tangy aroma.

Ingredients

You Need:

- 1 cup żur (fermented rye flour mixture), available at Polish specialty stores or homemade (see note below)
- 8 cups chicken or vegetable broth
- 1 onion, chopped
- 2 cloves garlic, minced
- 2 medium potatoes, peeled and diced
- 1 carrot, peeled and diced
- 1 parsnip, peeled and diced
- 1 cup cooked kielbasa or ham, diced (optional)
- 1 tablespoon butter or olive oil
- 1 bay leaf
- 1 teaspoon dried marjoram
- Salt and pepper to taste
- Sour cream and chopped fresh parsley or chives for serving

Directions

- **Prepare the Zur:** If using homemade żur, mix 1 cup of rye flour with 2 cups of warm water in a glass or ceramic container. Cover loosely with a clean cloth and let it sit at room temperature for 3-4 days, stirring occasionally, until it develops a sour aroma and starts to ferment. Strain the mixture through a fine-mesh sieve, discarding any solids, and refrigerate until ready to use.

- **Cook the Vegetables:** Heat the butter or olive oil over medium heat. Add the chopped onion and minced garlic to the pot and sauté until softened and fragrant, about 5 minutes. Add the diced potatoes, carrot, and parsnip to the pot and cook for another 5 minutes, stirring occasionally. Add broth and bring to a simmer.

- **Simmer the Soup:** Add the cooked kielbasa or ham (if using), bay leaf, dried marjoram, salt, and pepper to taste. Combine, then reduce the heat to low and let the soup simmer, uncovered, for about 30-40 minutes, or until the vegetables are tender and the flavors have melded together.

- **Add the Zur:** Gradually add the żur to the soup, stirring constantly to prevent lumps from forming. Continue to cook the soup for an additional 10-15 minutes, allowing the flavors to blend and the soup to thicken slightly.

Kapusniak (Cabbage Soup)

PREP TIME: 15 MIN COOKING TIME: 1 HOUR SERVES: 6-8 CALORIES PER SERVING: 200

Kapusniak is a traditional Polish cabbage soup that is hearty, flavorful, and perfect for warming up on a chilly day. This soup is often made with a variety of vegetables, including cabbage, carrots, potatoes, and onions, and sometimes includes meat such as sausage or bacon for added richness and flavor.

Ingredients

You Need:

- 1/2 head green cabbage, shredded
- 2 carrots, peeled and diced
- 2 potatoes, peeled and diced
- 1 onion, chopped
- 2 cloves garlic, minced
- 6 cups vegetable or chicken broth
- 1 can (14 ounces) diced tomatoes
- 1 tablespoon tomato paste
- 1 teaspoon paprika
- 1/2 teaspoon dried thyme
- Salt and pepper to taste
- 2 tablespoons olive oil or butter
- Chopped fresh parsley or dill for garnish (optional)
- Sour cream or yogurt for serving (optional)

Directions

- **Prepare the vegetables:** Shred the cabbage and dice the carrots and potatoes. Chop the onion and mince the garlic.

- **Saute the aromatics:** In a large pot, heat the olive oil or butter over medium heat. Add the chopped onion and minced garlic and sauté until softened and fragrant, about 5 minutes.

- **Add the vegetables:** Add the shredded cabbage, diced carrots, and diced potatoes to the pot with the sautéed onions and garlic. Stir to combine.

- **Simmer the soup:** Pour the vegetable or chicken broth into the pot with the vegetables. Add the diced tomatoes, tomato paste, paprika, dried thyme, salt, and pepper to taste. Stir well to combine. Bring the soup to a simmer over medium heat.

- **Cook the soup:** Once the soup is simmering, reduce the heat to low and let it cook, uncovered, for about 45 minutes to 1 hour, or until the vegetables are tender and the flavors have melded together.

- **Adjust the seasoning:** Taste the soup and adjust the seasoning as needed, adding more salt and pepper if desired.

Rosół (Chicken Broth)

PREP TIME: 15 MIN   COOKING TIME: 2-3 HOURS   SERVES: 6-8   CALORIES PER SERVING: 100

Rosół is a traditional Polish chicken broth that is often considered the ultimate comfort food. It's a simple yet flavorful soup made by simmering chicken meat and bones with vegetables and herbs, resulting in a clear and nourishing broth that is perfect for sipping on its own or used as a base for other soups and dishes.

Ingredients

You Need:
- 1 whole chicken (about 4 pounds), rinsed and patted dry
- 2 onions, peeled and halved
- 3 carrots, peeled and halved
- 2 celery stalks, halved
- 1 parsnip, peeled and halved
- 1 leek, trimmed and halved
- 6-8 cups water (enough to cover the chicken)
- 1 bay leaf
- 6-8 whole peppercorns
- Salt to taste
- Chopped fresh parsley for garnish (optional)
- Noodles

Directions

- **Prepare the chicken:** Place the whole chicken in a large pot and add enough water to cover it completely. Bring the water to a boil over high heat, then reduce the heat to low and let the chicken simmer gently for about 10 minutes. Skim off any foam or impurities that rise to the surface.
- **Add the vegetables:** Add the halved onions, carrots, celery stalks, parsnip, bay leaf, and whole peppercorns and leek to the pot. Add the noodles.
- **Simmer the broth:** Cover the pot partially with a lid and let the broth simmer gently over low heat for 2-3 hours, or until the chicken is cooked through and tender and the flavors have melded together. Skim off any excess fat or foam that accumulates on the surface of the broth during cooking.
- **Season the broth:** Once the broth is done simmering, remove the chicken from the pot and set it aside to cool slightly. Strain the broth through a fine-mesh sieve or cheesecloth into a clean pot or bowl, discarding the vegetables and aromatics. Season the broth with salt to taste.
- **Serve:** Once the chicken has cooled enough to handle, remove the meat from the bones and shred or chop it into bite-sized pieces. Ladle the hot Rosół into bowls and add some of the cooked chicken meat and noodles to each serving.
-

Zupa Grzybowa (Mushroom Soup)

PREP TIME: 15 MIN   COOKING TIME: 30 MIN   SERVES: 4-6   CALORIES PER SERVING: 100

Zupa Grzybowa, also known as Mushroom Soup, is a popular dish in Polish cuisine, especially during the autumn months when mushrooms are abundant in forests.

Ingredients

You Need:
- 1 whole chicken (about 4 pounds), rinsed and patted dry
- 2 onions, peeled and halved
- 3 carrots, peeled and halved
- 2 celery stalks, halved
- 1 parsnip, peeled and halved
- 1 leek, trimmed and halved
- 6-8 cups water (enough to cover the chicken)
- 1 bay leaf
- 6-8 whole peppercorns
- Salt to taste
- Chopped fresh parsley for garnish (optional)
- Noodles

Directions

- **Prepare the mushrooms:** Clean the mushrooms thoroughly and slice them into bite-sized pieces.

- **Saute the aromatics:** In a large pot, heat the olive oil or butter over medium heat. Add the chopped onion and minced garlic and sauté until softened and fragrant, about 5 minutes.

- **Cook the mushrooms:** Add the sliced mushrooms to the pot with the sautéed onions and garlic. Cook, stirring occasionally, until the mushrooms are browned and tender, about 8-10 minutes.

- **Add the potatoes and broth:** Add the diced potatoes to the pot with the cooked mushrooms, and pour in the vegetable or chicken broth. Stir in the bay leaf and dried thyme. Season with salt and pepper to taste.

- **Simmer the soup:** Bring the soup to a simmer over medium heat. Cover the pot partially with a lid and let the soup simmer gently for about 20-25 minutes or until the potatoes are tender and cooked through.

- **Adjust the seasoning:** Taste the soup and adjust the seasoning as needed, adding more salt and pepper if desired.

Chłodnik (Cold Beet Soup)

PREP TIME: 20 MIN   COOKING TIME: 30 MIN   SERVES: 4-6   CALORIES PER SERVING: 200

Chłodnik, also known as Cold Beet Soup, is a traditional Polish dish that dates back to the Middle Ages. Originally, it was made with fermented beets, but over time, the recipe evolved to include fresh beets and other seasonal vegetables.

Ingredients

You Need:

- 4 medium-sized beets, peeled and grated
- 1 cucumber, peeled and diced
- 2 cups plain yogurt or sour cream
- 4 cups cold vegetable or chicken broth
- 1 small bunch fresh dill, chopped
- 2 hard-boiled eggs, diced
- Salt and pepper to taste
- 1 tablespoon lemon juice (optional)
- 1 tablespoon honey or sugar (optional)
- Additional garnishes: extra dill, sliced radishes, chopped green onions

Directions

- **Prepare the beets:** If using raw beets, bring a pot of water to a boil and cook them for about 30 minutes or until tender. Once cooked, drain the beets, let them cool, and peel and grate them.

- **Mix the ingredients:** In a large bowl, combine the grated beets, diced cucumber, yogurt or sour cream, and cold broth. Stir well to combine.

- **Season the soup:** Add chopped fresh dill, diced hard-boiled eggs, salt, and pepper to taste. If desired, add a tablespoon of lemon juice for extra tanginess and a tablespoon of honey or sugar to balance the flavors.

- **Chill the soup:** Cover the bowl and refrigerate the soup for at least 2-3 hours to allow the flavors to meld together and for the soup to become cold.

Krupnik (Barley Soup)

PREP TIME: 15 MIN   COOKING TIME: 1 HR 30 MIN   SERVES: 6-8   CALORIES PER SERVING: 250

Krupnik is a traditional Polish barley soup that is hearty, comforting, and perfect for cold winter days. Krupnik is a staple dish in Polish cuisine and is enjoyed as a nourishing meal that warms both body and soul.

Ingredients

You Need:

- 1 cup pearl barley, rinsed
- 1 onion, chopped
- 2 carrots, peeled and diced
- 2 celery stalks, diced
- 2 cloves garlic, minced
- 8 cups vegetable or chicken broth
- 1 bay leaf
- 1 teaspoon dried thyme
- Salt and pepper to taste
- 2 tablespoons olive oil or butter
- Chopped fresh parsley or dill for garnish (optional)

Directions

- **Prepare the barley:** Rinse the pearl barley under cold water until the water runs clear. Drain and set aside.

- **Saute the aromatics:** Heat the olive oil or butter in a large pot over medium heat. Add the chopped onion, diced carrots, diced celery, and minced garlic to the pot. Saute until the vegetables are softened and fragrant, about 5-7 minutes.

- **Add the barley and broth:** Add the rinsed pearl barley to the pot with the sauteed vegetables. Pour in the vegetable or chicken broth. Add the bay leaf and dried thyme. Stir well to combine.

- **Simmer the soup:** Bring the soup to a simmer over medium heat. Reduce the heat to low, cover the pot partially with a lid, and let the soup simmer gently for about 1 hour, stirring occasionally, or until the barley is tender and cooked through.

- **Season the soup:** Taste the soup and season with salt and pepper to taste. Adjust the seasoning as needed.

You can also:

- Garnish with fresh dill or parsley before serving.

Zupa Pomidorowa (Tomato Soup)

PREP TIME: 10 MIN   COOKING TIME: 30 MIN   SERVES: 4-6   CALORIES PER SERVING: 150

Zupa Pomidorowa, or Tomato Soup, is a popular dish in Polish cuisine that is loved for its simplicity and comforting flavors. While tomatoes are not native to Poland, tomato soup has become a beloved part of Polish culinary tradition.

Ingredients

You Need:

- 2 tablespoons olive oil
- 1 onion, chopped
- 2 cloves garlic, minced
- 2 pounds fresh tomatoes, chopped (or 1 can (28 ounces) diced tomatoes)
- 4 cups vegetable or chicken broth
- 1 tablespoon tomato paste
- 1 teaspoon sugar
- 1/2 teaspoon dried basil
- 1/2 teaspoon dried oregano
- Salt and pepper to taste
- 1/4 cup heavy cream (optional)
- Chopped fresh basil or parsley for garnish (optional)

Directions

- **Saute the aromatics:** In a large pot, heat the olive oil over medium heat. Add the chopped onion and minced garlic to the pot and sauté until softened and fragrant, about 5 minutes.
- **Cook the tomatoes:** Add the chopped tomatoes to the pot with the sautéed onions and garlic. Cook, stirring occasionally, until the tomatoes begin to break down and release their juices, about 10 minutes.
- **Add the broth and seasonings:** Pour the vegetable or chicken broth into the pot with the cooked tomatoes, onions, and garlic. Stir in the tomato paste, sugar, dried basil, and dried oregano. Season with salt and pepper to taste.
- **Simmer the soup:** Bring the soup to a simmer over medium heat. Reduce the heat to low and let the soup simmer gently for about 15-20 minutes, allowing the flavors to meld together and the soup to thicken slightly.
- **Blend the soup (optional):** For a smoother texture, use an immersion blender to puree the soup directly in the pot until smooth. Alternatively, transfer the soup to a blender and blend in batches until smooth, then return it to the pot.
- **Finish the soup (optional):** Stir in the heavy cream, if using, to add richness and creaminess to the soup. Taste and adjust the seasoning as needed.

Kapusta Kiszoną (Sauerkraut Dish)

PREP TIME: 15 MIN   COOKING TIME: 45 MIN   SERVES: 6-8   CALORIES PER SERVING: 200

Kapusta Kiszoną, or Sauerkraut, is a traditional Polish dish that is popular during the colder months. Sauerkraut, fermented cabbage, is a staple ingredient in Polish cuisine and adds a unique tangy flavor to this hearty and comforting soup.

Ingredients

You Need:

- 2 cups sauerkraut, drained and rinsed
- 1 onion, chopped
- 2 cloves garlic, minced
- 2 carrots, peeled and diced
- 2 potatoes, peeled and diced
- 8 cups vegetable or chicken broth
- 1 bay leaf
- 1 teaspoon caraway seeds
- Salt and pepper to taste
- 2 tablespoons olive oil or butter
- Sour cream or yogurt for serving (optional)
- Chopped fresh parsley or dill for garnish (optional)

Directions

- **Prepare the sauerkraut:** Drain the sauerkraut and rinse it under cold water to remove excess brine. Squeeze out any excess moisture and set aside.
- **Saute the aromatics:** In a large pot, heat the olive oil or butter over medium heat. Add the chopped onion and minced garlic to the pot and sauté until softened and fragrant, about 5 minutes.
- **Add the vegetables:** Add the diced carrots and potatoes to the pot with the sautéed onions and garlic. Cook for another 5 minutes, stirring occasionally.
- **Add the sauerkraut and broth:** Add the drained and rinsed sauerkraut to the pot with the cooked vegetables. Pour in the vegetable or chicken broth. Add the bay leaf and caraway seeds. Stir well to combine.
- **Simmer:** Bring the soup to a simmer over medium heat. Cover the pot partially with a lid and let the soup simmer gently for about 30-40 minutes or until the vegetables are tender and cooked through.
- **Season:** Taste the soup and season with salt and pepper to taste. Adjust the seasoning as needed.

Śledź w Śmietanie (Herring in Cream Sauce)

PREP TIME: 15 MIN   COOKING TIME: 2-4 HOURS   SERVES: 4-6   CALORIES PER SERVING: 250

Śledź w Śmietanie, or Herring in Cream Sauce, is a classic Polish dish that is often served as an appetizer or part of a traditional Polish feast, especially during holidays and celebrations. Herring has been a staple ingredient in Polish cuisine for centuries

Ingredients

You Need:

- 1 pound herring fillets, cut into bite-sized pieces
- 1 onion, thinly sliced
- 1/2 cup sour cream
- 1/4 cup mayonnaise
- 2 tablespoons white vinegar
- 1 tablespoon granulated sugar
- 1 teaspoon Dijon mustard
- Salt and pepper to taste
- Chopped fresh dill for garnish (optional)
- Slices of rye bread or crackers for serving

Directions

- **Prepare the herring:** Rinse the herring fillets under cold water and pat them dry with paper towels. Cut the herring fillets into bite-sized pieces and place them in a shallow dish or bowl.

- **Marinate the herring:** In a separate bowl, whisk together the sour cream, mayonnaise, white vinegar, sugar, Dijon mustard, salt, and pepper until well combined. Pour the marinade over the herring fillets, making sure they are fully coated. Add the sliced onion to the dish and gently toss to combine. Cover the dish with plastic wrap and refrigerate for 2-4 hours to allow the flavors to meld together and the herring to marinate.

You can also:

- Add a dollop of mustard when serving for extra flavor and tanginess.

Flaki (Tripe Soup)

PREP TIME: 30 MIN   COOKING TIME: 2 HOURS   SERVES: 6-8   CALORIES PER SERVING: 300

Flaki, or Tripe Soup, is a traditional Polish dish that has been enjoyed for centuries. It is made from beef tripe, which is the edible lining of a cow's stomach. Flaki is considered a delicacy in Polish cuisine and is often served as a hearty and comforting soup, especially during cold winter months or as a hangover cure.

Ingredients

You Need:

- 1 pound beef tripe, cleaned and cut into small strips
- 1 onion, finely chopped
- 2 carrots, peeled and diced
- 2 celery stalks, diced
- 4 cups beef broth
- 4 cups water
- 1 bay leaf
- 1 teaspoon dried marjoram
- Salt and pepper to taste
- 2 tablespoons olive oil or butter
- Chopped fresh parsley for garnish (optional)
- Lemon wedges for serving (optional)

Directions

- **Prepare the tripe:** Rinse the beef tripe under cold water and pat it dry with paper towels. Cut the tripe into small strips and set aside.
- **Saute the aromatics:** In a large pot, heat the olive oil or butter over medium heat. Add the chopped onion, diced carrots, and diced celery to the pot. Saute until the vegetables are softened and fragrant, about 5-7 minutes.
- **Add the tripe:** Add the cleaned and cut beef tripe to the pot with the sauteed vegetables. Cook, stirring occasionally, until the tripe is slightly browned and cooked through about 10 minutes.
- **Simmer the soup:** Pour the beef broth and water into the pot with the cooked tripe and vegetables. Add the bay leaf and dried marjoram. Season with salt and pepper to taste. Bring the soup to a simmer over medium heat.
- **Cook until tender:** Reduce the heat to low, cover the pot partially with a lid, and let the soup simmer gently for about 1.5 to 2 hours or until the tripe is tender and cooked through. Stir occasionally to prevent sticking and ensure even cooking
- **Adjust seasoning:** Taste the soup and adjust the seasoning with salt and pepper, if needed.

Grochówka (Split Pea Soup)

PREP TIME: 10 MIN   COOKING TIME: 1 HR 30   SERVES: 6-8   CALORIES PER SERVING: 250

Grochówka, or Slit Pea Soup, is a beloved Polish dish that has been enjoyed for generations. It has humble origins and is often associated with Polish soldiers, who would prepare it using simple ingredients like dried peas, potatoes, and smoked bacon during military campaigns.

Ingredients

You Need:

- 1 cup dried green peas, rinsed and soaked overnight
- 1 onion, chopped
- 2 carrots, peeled and diced
- 2 celery stalks, diced
- 2 potatoes, peeled and diced
- 4 cups vegetable or chicken broth
- 4 cups water
- 4 slices smoked bacon, chopped
- 1 bay leaf
- 1 teaspoon dried thyme
- Salt and pepper to taste
- Chopped fresh parsley for garnish (optional)
- Crusty bread or croutons for serving

Directions

- **Prepare the peas:** Rinse the dried green peas under cold water and soak them in a bowl of water overnight to soften.
- **Saute the aromatics:** In a large pot, cook the chopped bacon over medium heat until crispy and browned. Remove the bacon from the pot and set aside. In the same pot with the bacon drippings, add the chopped onion, diced carrots, and diced celery. Saute until the vegetables are softened and fragrant, about 5-7 minutes.
- **Add the peas and potatoes:** Drain the soaked peas and add them to the pot with the sauteed vegetables. Stir in the diced potatoes.
- **Simmer the soup:** Pour the vegetable or chicken broth and water into the pot with the peas and vegetables. Add the bay leaf and dried thyme. Season with salt and pepper to taste and simmer on medium heat.
- **Cook until tender:** Reduce the heat to low, cover the pot partially with a lid, and let the soup simmer gently for about 1 to 1.5 hours, or until the peas and vegetables are tender and cooked through. Stir occasionally to prevent sticking and ensure even cooking.
- **Adjust seasoning:** Taste the soup and adjust the seasoning with salt and pepper, if needed.

Kapusniak z Grochem (Cabbage and Pea Soup)

PREP TIME: 15 MIN   COOKING TIME: 1 HR 30   SERVES: 6-8   CALORIES PER SERVING: 250

Kapusniak z Grochem, or Cabbage and Pea Soup, is a traditional Polish dish that combines the flavors of sweet cabbage and tender peas in a hearty and satisfying soup. This dish is often enjoyed during the colder months, as it provides warmth and comfort on chilly days.

Ingredients
You Need:
- 1 cup dried green peas, rinsed and soaked overnight
- 1 onion, chopped
- 2 carrots, peeled and diced
- 2 celery stalks, diced
- 1 small head of cabbage, shredded
- 4 cups vegetable or chicken broth
- 4 cups water
- 4 slices bacon, chopped
- 2 tablespoons olive oil or butter
- 1 bay leaf
- 1 teaspoon dried thyme
- Salt and pepper to taste
- Chopped fresh parsley for garnish (optional)
- Crusty bread for serving

Directions
- **Prepare the peas:** Rinse the dried green peas under cold water and soak them in a bowl of water overnight to soften.
- **Saute the aromatics:** In a large pot, cook the chopped bacon over medium heat until crispy and browned. Remove the bacon from the pot and set aside. In the same pot with the bacon drippings, add the chopped onion, diced carrots, and diced celery. Saute until the vegetables are softened and fragrant, about 5-7 minutes.
- **Add the cabbage:** Add the shredded cabbage to the pot with the sauteed vegetables. Cook, stirring occasionally, until the cabbage is wilted and tender, about 10 minutes
- **Add the peas and broth:** Drain the soaked peas and add them to the pot with the cooked vegetables. Pour in the vegetable or chicken broth and water. Add the bay leaf and dried thyme. Season with salt and pepper to taste.
- **Simmer the soup:** Bring the soup to a simmer over medium heat. Reduce the heat to low, cover the pot partially with a lid, and let the soup simmer gently for about 1 to 1.5 hours or until the peas and vegetables are tender and cooked through. Stir occasionally to prevent sticking and ensure even cooking. Taste the soup and adjust the seasoning with salt and pepper, if needed.

Zupa Fasolowa (Bean Soup)

PREP TIME: 10 MIN   COOKING TIME: 1 HR 30   SERVES: 6-8   CALORIES PER SERVING: 250

Zupa Fasolowa, or Bean Soup, is a traditional Polish dish that has been enjoyed for generations. Beans have been a staple ingredient in Polish cuisine for centuries, and this soup showcases their rich flavor and hearty texture.

Ingredients

You Need:

- 1 cup dried white beans (navy beans or cannellini beans), rinsed and soaked overnight
- 1 onion, chopped
- 2 carrots, peeled and diced
- 2 celery stalks, diced
- 2 cloves garlic, minced
- 4 cups vegetable or chicken broth
- 4 cups water
- 2 bay leaves
- 1 teaspoon dried thyme
- Salt and pepper to taste
- 2 tablespoons olive oil or butter
- Chopped fresh parsley for garnish (optional)
- Crusty bread for serving

Directions

- **Prepare the beans:** Rinse the dried white beans under cold water and soak them in a bowl of water overnight to soften.
- **Saute the aromatics:** In a large pot, heat the olive oil or butter over medium heat. Add the chopped onion, diced carrots, and diced celery to the pot. Saute until the vegetables are softened and fragrant, about 5-7 minutes. Add the minced garlic and saute for another 1-2 minutes.
- **Add the beans and broth:** Drain the soaked beans and add them to the pot with the sauteed vegetables. Pour in the vegetable or chicken broth and water. Add the bay leaves and dried thyme. Season with salt and pepper to taste.
- **Simmer the soup:** Bring the soup to a boil over medium-high heat. Reduce the heat to low, cover the pot partially with a lid, and let the soup simmer gently for about 1 to 1.5 hours or until the beans are tender and cooked through. Stir occasionally to prevent sticking and ensure even cooking.
- **Mash some of the beans (optional):** Use a potato masher to mash some of the beans directly in the pot. This will help thicken the soup and give it a creamy texture.
- **Adjust seasoning:** Taste the soup and adjust the seasoning with salt and pepper, if needed.

Kluski do Rosołu (Noodles for Chicken Soup)

PREP TIME: 10 MIN   COOKING TIME: 1 HR 30   SERVES: 6-8   CALORIES PER SERVING: 250

Kluski do Rosołu, or Noodles for Chicken Soup, is a simple and comforting dish that is enjoyed in Polish households throughout the year. Kluski do Rosołu is loved for its simplicity, warmth, and nourishing qualities, making it a popular choice for a cozy meal.

Ingredients

You Need:

For the noodles

- 2 cups all-purpose flour
- 2 eggs
- 1/2 teaspoon salt
- Water, as needed

For the soup

- 8 cups chicken or beef broth (rosół)
- 1 onion, chopped
- 2 carrots, peeled and diced
- 2 celery stalks, diced
- 2 cloves garlic, minced
- 1 bay leaf
- Salt and pepper to taste
- Chopped fresh parsley for garnish (optional)

Directions

- **Make the noodles:** In a large mixing bowl, combine the all-purpose flour, eggs, and salt. Add water a little at a time, and knead the dough until it comes together and forms a smooth ball. The dough should be firm but pliable. If it's too dry, add more water; if it's too sticky, add more flour. Cover the dough with a clean kitchen towel and let it rest for about 10 minutes.
- **Roll out the noodles:** On a floured surface, roll out the dough to about 1/8-inch thickness. Use a sharp knife or pizza cutter to cut the dough into thin strips to form noodles. You can make them as long or short as you prefer.
- **Prepare the soup:** In a large pot, heat the chicken or beef broth over medium heat until simmering. Add the chopped onion, diced carrots, diced celery, minced garlic, and bay leaf to the pot. Season with salt and pepper to taste. Let the soup simmer gently for about 15-20 minutes or until the vegetables are tender and cooked through.
- **Cook the noodles:** Carefully drop the homemade noodles into the simmering soup, one by one, making sure they are evenly distributed. Cook the noodles in the soup for about 5-7 minutes or until they are tender and cooked through. Stir the soup gently to prevent the noodles from sticking to the bottom of the pot.

CHAPTER THREE

APPETIZERS (PRZEKĄSKI)

Pasztet (Liver Pate)

PREP TIME: 20 MIN　**COOKING TIME: 1 HR 30**　**SERVES: 2 CUPS**　**CAL PER SERVING: 200**

Pasztet, or Liver Pate, is a popular Polish dish that is enjoyed as an appetizer or spread. It is often served on bread or crackers and is a staple at gatherings and celebrations.

Ingredients

You Need:

- 1 pound chicken or pork liver, trimmed and cleaned
- 1 onion, chopped
- 2 cloves garlic, minced
- 4 tablespoons butter
- 2 eggs
- 1/4 cup heavy cream
- 1 teaspoon dried thyme
- 1/2 teaspoon ground allspice
- Salt and pepper to taste
- 2 slices of bread, crusts removed
- 2 tablespoons brandy or cognac (optional)
- Butter or oil for greasing the baking dish

Directions

- **Preheat the oven:** Preheat your oven to 350°F (175°C).
- **Saute the aromatics:** In a skillet, melt 2 tablespoons of butter over medium heat. Add the chopped onion and minced garlic to the skillet and saute until softened and fragrant, about 5-7 minutes. Remove from heat and set aside.
- **Prepare the liver:** Rinse the chicken or pork liver under cold water and pat dry with paper towels. Cut the liver into small pieces and place them in a food processor.
- **Blend the liver:** Pulse the liver in the food processor until finely chopped. Add the sauteed onion and garlic mixture to the food processor, along with the eggs, heavy cream, dried thyme, ground allspice, salt, and pepper. Blend until smooth and well combined.
- **Soak the bread:** Tear the slices of bread into small pieces and place them in a bowl. Pour enough water over the bread to cover it, then let it soak for a few minutes until softened. Squeeze out any excess water from the bread and add it to the liver mixture in the food processor. Blend again
- **Grease the baking dish:** Grease a baking dish with butter or oil to prevent the pate from sticking.
- **Bake the pate:** Transfer the liver mixture to the greased baking dish and smooth the top with a spatula. Cover the dish with aluminum foil and bake in the preheated oven for about 1 hour, or until the pate is set and cooked through.
- **Cool and refrigerate:** Once baked, remove the pate from the oven and let it cool to room temperature. Then, cover the dish with plastic wrap and refrigerate for at least 2 hours, or until the pate is chilled and firm.

Śledź w Oleju (Marinated Herring)

PREP TIME: 20 MIN **COOKING TIME: 0** **SERVES: 4-6** **CALORIES PER SERVING: 200**

Śledź w Oleju, or Marinated Herring, is a traditional Polish dish that is enjoyed as a flavorful appetizer or side dish. Herring has been a staple in Polish cuisine for centuries, and marinating it in a mixture of vinegar, oil, and spices enhances its flavor and preserves it for longer storage.

Ingredients

You Need:

- 4-6 herring fillets, cleaned and deboned
- 1 onion, thinly sliced
- 2 tablespoons granulated sugar
- 1 cup white vinegar
- 1/2 cup water
- 1/4 cup vegetable oil
- 1 bay leaf
- 5 whole peppercorns
- 5 whole allspice berries
- 2 cloves
- 1 teaspoon mustard seeds
- 1 teaspoon dried dill
- Salt and pepper to taste
- Fresh dill and lemon slices for garnish (optional)

Directions

- **Prepare the herring:** Rinse the herring fillets under cold water and pat them dry with paper towels. Cut the fillets into bite-sized pieces and place them in a shallow dish or glass container.

- **Make the marinade:** In a saucepan, combine the sliced onion, granulated sugar, white vinegar, water, vegetable oil, bay leaf, peppercorns, allspice berries, cloves, mustard seeds, dried dill, salt, and pepper. Bring the mixture to a simmer over medium heat, stirring occasionally, until the sugar is dissolved and the flavors are well combined. Remove the marinade from heat and let it cool slightly.

- **Marinate the herring:** Pour the warm marinade over the herring fillets in the dish, making sure they are completely covered. Cover the dish with plastic wrap or a lid and refrigerate for 12 to 24 hours, allowing the herring to marinate and absorb the flavors.

You can also:

- Garnish your dish with fresh dill and lemon slices.

Kiełbasa (Polish Sausage)

PREP TIME: 20 MIN   COOKING TIME: 30 MIN   SERVES: 6-8   CALORIES PER SERVING: 300

Kiełbasa, a traditional Polish sausage, is a beloved dish that holds a special place in Polish cuisine and culture. Dating back centuries, kiełbasa has been a staple food in Poland, enjoyed by people of all ages and backgrounds.

Ingredients

You Need:

- 2 pounds ground pork (or a combination of pork and beef)
- 2 teaspoons salt
- 1 teaspoon black pepper
- 1 teaspoon garlic powder
- 1 teaspoon paprika
- 1/2 teaspoon ground marjoram
- 1/2 teaspoon ground mustard seed
- 1/4 teaspoon ground allspice
- 1/4 teaspoon ground coriander
- 1/4 teaspoon ground nutmeg
- Hog casings (optional, for stuffing)
- Vegetable oil (for cooking)

Directions

- **Prepare the meat mixture:** In a large mixing bowl, combine the ground pork with salt, black pepper, garlic powder, paprika, marjoram, mustard seed, allspice, coriander, and nutmeg. Use your hands to mix the spices evenly into the meat mixture. Cover the bowl with plastic wrap and refrigerate for at least 2 hours, or overnight, to allow the flavors to meld.
- **Prepare the casings (if using):** If using hog casings to make traditional sausage links, rinse them thoroughly under cold water to remove any salt and debris. Soak the casings in warm water for about 30 minutes to soften them before stuffing.
- **Stuff the sausage:** If using casings, attach one end securely to the nozzle of a sausage stuffer or a piping bag. Carefully feed the meat mixture into the casing, gently pushing it through to fill the casing evenly. Twist the filled casing into desired lengths to form sausage links. Alternatively, if not using casings, shape the meat mixture into sausage patties or logs by hand.
- **Rest the sausage (if using casings):** Once the sausage is stuffed or shaped, let it rest in the refrigerator for at least 30 minutes to allow the flavors to develop and the sausage to firm up.
- **Cook the sausage:** Heat a skillet or grill over medium heat and lightly oil the surface to prevent sticking. Cook the sausage links or patties for about 5-7 minutes on each side or until browned and cooked through. If unsure, use a meat thermometer to ensure the internal temperature reaches 160°F (71°C).

Sałatka Jarzynowa (Polish Vegetable Salad)

PREP TIME: 30 MIN   COOKING TIME: 20 MIN   SERVES: 6-8   CALORIES PER SERVING: 200

Sałatka Jarzynowa, or Polish Vegetable Salad, is a classic dish enjoyed throughout Poland, especially during holidays and family gatherings. This hearty salad is known for its vibrant colors, fresh flavors, and creamy texture.

Ingredients

You Need:

- 4 medium potatoes, peeled and diced
- 4 carrots, peeled and diced
- 2 large eggs
- 1 cup frozen peas, thawed
- 1 cup diced pickles (Polish dill pickles preferred)
- 1 medium apple, peeled and diced
- 1/2 cup diced cooked ham or cooked chicken breast (optional)
- 1/2 cup mayonnaise
- 2 tablespoons sour cream
- 1 tablespoon mustard
- Salt and pepper to taste
- Chopped fresh dill or parsley for garnish (optional)

Directions

- **Boil the potatoes and carrots:** In a large pot, bring salted water to a boil. Add the diced potatoes and carrots to the boiling water and cook until tender, about 10-12 minutes. Drain the cooked vegetables and let them cool completely.
- **Boil the eggs:** Place the eggs in a separate pot and cover them with water. Bring the water to a boil, then reduce the heat to a simmer and cook the eggs for 8-10 minutes. Remove the eggs from the pot and transfer them to a bowl of cold water to cool. Once cooled, peel the eggs and dice them.
- **Prepare the salad:** In a large mixing bowl, combine the cooked and cooled potatoes, carrots, diced eggs, thawed peas, diced pickles, diced apples, and cooked ham or chicken (if using).
- **Make the dressing:** In a small bowl, whisk together the mayonnaise, sour cream, and mustard until smooth and well combined. Season the dressing with salt and pepper to taste.
- **Dress the salad:** Pour the prepared dressing over the salad ingredients in the mixing bowl. Gently toss them together.
- **Chill the salad:** Cover the bowl with plastic wrap or a lid and refrigerate for at least 1 hour or until chilled and the flavors have melded together.

Kulebiak (Fish Pie)

PREP TIME: 30 MIN   COOKING TIME: 1 HOUR   SERVES: 6-8   CALORIES PER SERVING: 350

Kulebiak, also known as Coulibiac or Russian Fish Pie, is a traditional Eastern European dish with roots in Russian and Polish cuisine. Kulebiak is often served as a main course during special occasions and celebrations, and its name is derived from the Russian word "kulebyaka," which originally referred to a type of pie filled with meat or fish.

Ingredients

You Need:

For the pastry dough

- 2 cups all-purpose flour
- 1 teaspoon salt
- 1/2 cup unsalted butter, chilled and cubed
- 1/2 cup cold water

- **For the filling**
- 1 pound white fish fillets (such as cod or haddock), cooked and flaked
- 1 cup cooked white rice
- 2 hard-boiled eggs, chopped
- 1 onion, finely chopped
- 2 cloves garlic, minced
- 1 cup sliced mushrooms
- 1/2 cup chopped fresh dill
- Salt and pepper to taste
- 2 tablespoons olive oil
- 1 egg, beaten (for egg wash)

Directions

- **Prepare the pastry dough:** In a large mixing bowl, combine the flour and salt. Add the chilled cubed butter to the flour mixture and use a pastry cutter or your fingers to rub the butter into the flour until it resembles coarse crumbs. Gradually add the cold water, a little at a time, and mix until a dough forms. Shape the dough into a ball, wrap it in plastic wrap, and refrigerate for at least 30 minutes.
- **Prepare the filling:** Heat the olive oil in a skillet over medium heat. Add the chopped onion and minced garlic and cook until softened and translucent, about 5 minutes. Add the sliced mushrooms and cook until they release their juices and become tender, about 5-7 minutes more. Remove the skillet from heat and let the mixture cool slightly.
- **Assemble the pie:** Preheat your oven to 375°F (190°C). On a lightly floured surface, roll out the chilled pastry dough into a large rectangle about 1/4 inch thick. Carefully transfer the rolled dough to a parchment-lined baking sheet.
- **Layer the filling**
- **Fold and seal the pie:** Brush the top of the pie with beaten egg for a golden finish.
- **Bake the pie:** Place the assembled Kulebiak in the preheated oven and bake for 40-45 minutes, or until the pastry is golden brown and cooked through.

Placki Ziemniaczane (Potato Pancakes)

PREP TIME: 20 MIN   COOKING TIME: 20 MIN   SERVES: 10-12   CALORIES PER SERVING: 150

Potato pancakes, known as Placki Ziemniaczane in Polish, have been a popular dish in Poland for centuries. They are traditionally served with sour cream or applesauce and are enjoyed as a comforting and hearty meal.

Ingredients

You Need:

- 4 large potatoes, peeled
- 1 small onion, finely grated
- 2 eggs, lightly beaten
- 4 tablespoons all-purpose flour
- 1 teaspoon salt
- 1/2 teaspoon black pepper
- Vegetable oil, for frying
- Sour cream or applesauce, for serving (optional)
- Chopped fresh chives or parsley, for garnish (optional)

Directions

- **Grate the potatoes:** Using a box grater or a food processor fitted with a grating attachment, grate the peeled potatoes. Place the grated potatoes in a clean kitchen towel or cheesecloth and squeeze out as much liquid as possible.
- **Combine the ingredients:** In a large mixing bowl, combine the grated potatoes, finely grated onion, beaten eggs, all-purpose flour, salt, and black pepper. Mix well until all ingredients are evenly combined.
- **Heat the oil:** In a large skillet or frying pan, heat enough vegetable oil to cover the bottom of the pan over medium heat until hot but not smoking.
- **Fry the pancakes:** Scoop about 1/4 cup of the potato mixture and drop it into the hot oil, flattening it slightly with the back of a spoon to form a pancake shape. Repeat with the remaining potato mixture, making sure not to overcrowd the pan. Cook the pancakes for 3-4 minutes on each side or until golden brown and crispy.
- **Drain and serve:** Once cooked, transfer the potato pancakes to a plate lined with paper towels to drain any excess oil.

Rolady (Stuffed Beef Rolls)

PREP TIME: 30 MIN   COOKING TIME: 1 HOUR   SERVES: 6-8   CALORIES PER SERVING: 400

Rolady, also known as Polish Stuffed Beef Rolls, are a classic dish in Polish cuisine, often enjoyed during festive occasions and family gatherings. These flavorful beef rolls are filled with a savory mixture of vegetables, herbs, and sometimes bacon, creating a hearty and satisfying meal.

Ingredients

You Need:

For the beef rolls
- 6-8 thin beef steaks or slices (such as flank steak or sirloin)
- Salt and pepper to taste
- 1 onion, finely chopped
- 2 cloves garlic, minced
- 1 carrot, grated
- 1 celery stalk, finely chopped
- 4 slices bacon, chopped (optional)
- 1/2 cup bread crumbs
- 1/4 cup chopped fresh parsley
- 1 egg, lightly beaten
- 1 tablespoon vegetable oil

For the sauce
- 2 cups beef broth
- 1/2 cup dry red wine (optional)
- 2 tablespoons all-purpose flour
- Salt and pepper to taste

Directions

- **Prepare the beef rolls:** Season the beef steaks with salt and pepper on both sides. In a large mixing bowl, combine the chopped onion, minced garlic, grated carrot, chopped celery, chopped bacon (if using), bread crumbs, chopped parsley, and beaten egg.
- **Assemble the rolls:** Lay out the beef steaks on a flat surface and divide the filling mixture evenly among them, spreading it over the surface of each steak. Roll up the steaks tightly to enclose the filling, securing them with toothpicks or kitchen twine if necessary.
- **Brown the rolls:** In a large skillet or frying pan, heat the vegetable oil over medium-high heat. Add the beef rolls to the skillet and cook for 2-3 minutes on each side or until browned on all sides. Remove the rolls from the skillet and set aside.
- **Make the sauce:** In the same skillet, pour in the beef broth and red wine (if using), scraping up any browned bits from the bottom of the pan. Bring the mixture to a simmer. In a small bowl, whisk together the all-purpose flour with a bit of water to make a slurry. Gradually whisk the flour mixture into the simmering broth until thickened. Season the sauce with salt and pepper to taste.
- **Simmer the rolls:** Return the browned beef rolls to the skillet with the sauce, spooning some of the sauce over the top of each roll. Cover the skillet with a lid and simmer the rolls over low heat for 45-60 minutes or until the beef is tender and cooked through.

Naleśniki (Polish Crepes)

PREP TIME: 10 MIN   COOKING TIME: 20 MIN   SERVES: 10-12   CALORIES PER SERVING: 100

Naleśniki, or Polish Crepes, are a versatile and beloved dish in Polish cuisine. They can be enjoyed as a sweet treat filled with fruit preserves or sweet cheese, or as a savory meal filled with meat, cheese, or vegetables.

Ingredients

You Need:
- 1 cup all-purpose flour
- 2 eggs
- 1 cup milk
- 1/4 cup water
- 2 tablespoons melted butter, plus extra for greasing the pan
- Pinch of salt
- 1 teaspoon sugar (optional, for sweet crepes)
- Fillings of your choice, such as fruit preserves, sweet cheese, Nutella, cooked meats, cheese, or vegetables

Directions

- **Prepare the batter:** In a large mixing bowl, whisk together the flour, eggs, milk, water, melted butter, salt, and sugar (if using) until smooth and well combined. The batter should have a consistency similar to heavy cream. If it's too thick, you can add a little more milk or water to thin it out.

- **Let the batter rest:** Cover the bowl with plastic wrap and let the batter rest at room temperature for at least 30 minutes or up to 1 hour. This allows the gluten in the flour to relax and the batter to thicken slightly.

- **Cook the crepes:** Heat a non-stick skillet or crepe pan over medium heat. Lightly grease the pan with melted butter or cooking spray. Pour about 1/4 cup of the batter into the center of the pan and immediately tilt and rotate the pan to spread the batter thinly and evenly across the bottom.

- **Cook the crepes:** Cook the crepe for about 1-2 minutes, or until the edges start to lift and the bottom is lightly golden brown. Use a spatula to carefully flip the crepe and cook for an additional 1-2 minutes on the other side until lightly golden brown. Repeat with the remaining batter, greasing the pan as needed between crepes.

Pasztet Drobiowy (Chicken Liver Pate)

PREP TIME: 15 MIN **COOKING TIME: 20 MIN** **SERVES: 8** **CALORIES PER SERVING: 200**

Pasztet drobiowy, or Chicken Liver Pate, is a classic Polish appetizer enjoyed as a spread on bread or crackers. It is often served as part of a charcuterie board or as an accompaniment to meals during special occasions and celebrations

Ingredients

You Need:

- 1 pound chicken livers, trimmed and cleaned
- 1 onion, finely chopped
- 2 cloves garlic, minced
- 4 tablespoons unsalted butter
- 2 tablespoons brandy or cognac (optional)
- 1/4 teaspoon dried thyme
- 1/4 teaspoon dried rosemary
- Salt and pepper to taste
- 2 tablespoons heavy cream or sour cream
- Toasted bread or crackers, for serving

Directions

- **Cook the chicken livers:** Melt 2 tablespoons of butter in a large skillet or frying pan over medium heat. Add the chopped onion and minced garlic to the skillet and cook until softened and translucent, about 5 minutes. Add the chicken livers to the skillet and cook for 8-10 minutes, or until they are cooked through but still slightly pink in the center. Remove the skillet from heat and let the mixture cool slightly.

- **Blend the mixture:** Transfer the cooked chicken livers, onions, and garlic to a food processor or blender. Add the remaining 2 tablespoons of butter, brandy, or cognac (if using), dried thyme, dried rosemary, salt, and pepper to taste. Blend the mixture until smooth and creamy, scraping down the sides of the bowl as needed.

- **Add the cream:** Gradually add the heavy cream or sour cream to the chicken liver mixture and blend until well combined. Taste and adjust seasoning if necessary.

- **Chill the pate:** Transfer the chicken liver pate to a small serving dish or ramekin. Cover with plastic wrap and refrigerate for at least 2 hours or until firm.

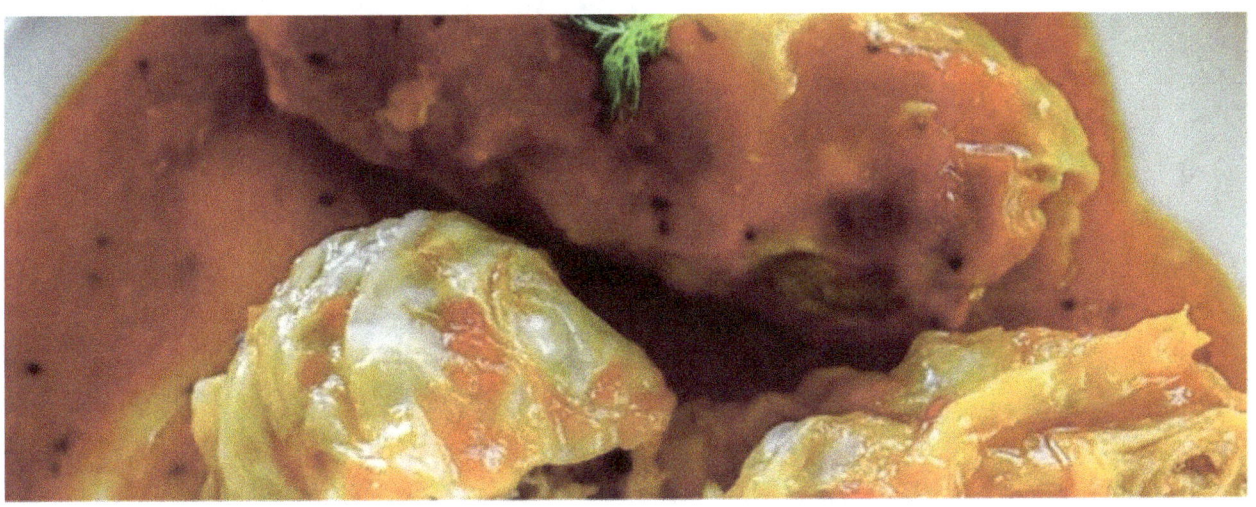

Gołąbki (Stuffed Cabbage Rolls)

PREP TIME: 30 MIN   COOKING TIME: 1 HR 30   SERVES: 8-10   CALORIES PER SERVING: 250

Gołąbki, meaning "little pigeons" in Polish, are a traditional Polish dish enjoyed for generations. Despite their name, these cabbage rolls have nothing to do with pigeons; rather, they are made with cabbage leaves wrapped around a filling of ground meat, rice, and spices, then baked in a flavorful tomato sauce.

Ingredients

You Need:

For the cabbage rolls
- 1 large head of cabbage
- 1 pound ground beef or pork
- 1/2 cup cooked white rice
- 1 onion, finely chopped
- 2 cloves garlic, minced
- 1 egg, lightly beaten
- 1 teaspoon dried thyme
- 1 teaspoon dried oregano
- Salt and pepper to taste

For the tomato sauce
- 2 cups tomato sauce or crushed tomatoes
- 1 tablespoon brown sugar
- 1 tablespoon apple cider vinegar
- 1 teaspoon paprika
- Salt and pepper to taste

Directions

- **Prepare the cabbage:** Bring a large pot of water to a boil. Core the cabbage and carefully remove the leaves, being careful not to tear them. Blanch the cabbage leaves in the boiling water for 2-3 minutes or until they are softened and pliable. Remove the leaves from the water and let them cool slightly.
- **Make the filling:** In a large mixing bowl, combine the ground beef or pork, cooked rice, chopped onion, minced garlic, beaten egg, dried thyme, dried oregano, salt, and pepper. Mix well until all ingredients are evenly combined.
- **Assemble the cabbage rolls:** Place a spoonful of the filling mixture onto the center of each cabbage leaf. Fold the sides of the leaf over the filling, then roll it up tightly to enclose the filling. Repeat with the remaining cabbage leaves and filling.
- **Make the tomato sauce:** In a separate bowl, combine the tomato sauce or crushed tomatoes, brown sugar, apple cider vinegar, paprika, salt, and pepper. Mix well to combine.
- **Arrange the cabbage rolls:** Preheat your oven to 350°F (175°C). Pour a small amount of the tomato sauce into the bottom of a baking dish. Place the cabbage rolls seam-side down in the dish, packing them tightly together.
- **Bake the rolls:** Pour the remaining tomato sauce over the top of the cabbage rolls, covering them evenly. Cover the baking dish with aluminum foil and bake in the preheated oven for 1 hour, or until the cabbage rolls are cooked through and the sauce is bubbling.

Jajka Faszerowane (Stuffed Eggs)

PREP TIME: 20 MIN   **COOKING TIME: 10 MIN**   **SERVES: 12**   **CALORIES PER SERVING: 60**

Jajka Faszerowane, or Stuffed Eggs, are a popular appetizer in Polish cuisine, often served at parties, gatherings, and holidays. These delicious stuffed eggs are filled with a creamy and flavorful mixture of egg yolks, mayonnaise, mustard, and seasonings, making them a tasty and satisfying bite-sized treat.

Ingredients

You Need:

- 6 hard-boiled eggs, peeled
- 2 tablespoons mayonnaise
- 1 teaspoon Dijon mustard
- 1 teaspoon white vinegar or lemon juice
- Salt and pepper to taste
- Paprika or chopped fresh chives for garnish

Directions

- **Prepare the eggs:** Cut the hard-boiled eggs in half lengthwise. Carefully remove the yolks and place them in a small mixing bowl. Arrange the egg white halves on a serving platter.

- **Make the filling:** Mash the egg yolks with a fork until smooth and creamy. Add the mayonnaise, Dijon mustard, white vinegar or lemon juice, salt, and pepper to the bowl with the mashed yolks. Mix well until all ingredients are combined, and the filling is smooth.

- **Fill the eggs:** Spoon or pipe the yolk mixture into the hollowed-out egg white halves, dividing it evenly among them.

- **Garnish:** Sprinkle the stuffed eggs with paprika or chopped fresh chives for a pop of color and flavor.

Paszteciki (Mini Pastries)

PREP TIME: 30 MIN   COOKING TIME: 20 MIN   SERVES: 12   CALORIES PER SERVING: 100

Paszteciki are a popular Polish snack or appetizer, traditionally filled with a savory mixture of mushrooms, onions, and meat or fish, then deep-fried until golden and crispy. These delicious mini pastries are often enjoyed as street food or served as a starter during family gatherings and celebrations.

Ingredients

You Need:

For the dough
- 1 1/2 cups all-purpose flour
- 1/2 teaspoon salt
- 1/2 cup warm water
- 2 tablespoons vegetable oil

For the filling
- 1 tablespoon butter
- 1 small onion, finely chopped
- 8 ounces mushrooms, finely chopped
- 1/2 cup cooked meat or fish (such as ground beef, chicken, or salmon)
- Salt and pepper to taste
- 1/4 cup sour cream or cream cheese

For frying
- Vegetable oil for deep-frying

Directions

- **Prepare the dough:** In a large mixing bowl, combine the flour and salt. Gradually add the warm water and vegetable oil, stirring until a smooth dough forms. Knead the dough on a floured surface for a few minutes until it is soft and elastic. Cover the dough with a clean kitchen towel and let it rest for 10-15 minutes.
- **Make the filling:** In a skillet or frying pan, melt the butter over medium heat. Add the chopped onion and cook until softened and translucent, about 5 minutes. Add the chopped mushrooms to the skillet and cook until they release their moisture and become golden brown, about 8-10 minutes. Stir in the cooked meat or fish and season with salt and pepper to taste. Remove the skillet from heat and let the mixture cool slightly. Once cooled, stir in the sour cream or cream cheese until well combined.
- **Assemble the paszteciki:** Divide the dough into 12 equal portions. Roll out each portion into a small circle or oval shape, about 1/8 inch thick. Place a spoonful of the filling onto one half of each dough circle, leaving a border around the edges. Fold the other half of the dough over the filling to enclose it, then crimp the edges with a fork to seal.
- **Fry the paszteciki:** In a deep fryer or large pot, heat vegetable oil to 350°F (175°C). Carefully place the filled paszteciki into the hot oil, a few at a time, and fry until golden brown and crispy, about 3-4 minutes per side. Use a slotted spoon to transfer the fried paszteciki to a plate lined with paper towels to cool down and remove excess oil.

Placki Drożdżowe (Yeast Pancakes)

PREP TIME: 1 HR 30   COOKING TIME: 15 MIN   SERVES: 12   CALORIES PER SERVING: 200

Placki Drożdżowe, or Yeast Pancakes, are a traditional Polish dish enjoyed for breakfast or as a sweet treat. Unlike traditional pancakes, which are made with baking powder or baking soda, yeast pancakes are leavened with active dry yeast, giving them a light and fluffy texture.

Ingredients

- 1 packet (2 1/4 teaspoons) active dry yeast
- 1 cup warm milk (110°F/45°C)
- 2 tablespoons granulated sugar
- 2 cups all-purpose flour
- 2 large eggs
- 1/4 teaspoon salt
- 2 tablespoons unsalted butter, melted
- Vegetable oil for frying
- Powdered sugar, fruit preserves, or maple syrup for serving

Directions

- **Activate the yeast:** In a small bowl, dissolve the active dry yeast and granulated sugar in the warm milk. Let the mixture sit for 5-10 minutes or until frothy and bubbly.
- **Make the batter:** In a large mixing bowl, combine the flour and salt. Make a well in the center of the flour mixture and pour in the activated yeast mixture, beaten eggs, and melted butter. Stir the ingredients together until a smooth batter forms. The batter should be thick but pourable. If it's too thick, you can add a little more warm milk to thin it out.
- **Let the batter rise:** Cover the bowl with plastic wrap or a clean kitchen towel and let the batter rise in a warm place for 1 hour or until doubled in size. During this time, the yeast will work its magic, and the batter will become light and airy.
- **Fry the pancakes:** Heat a non-stick skillet or griddle over medium heat and lightly grease it with vegetable oil. Pour about 1/4 cup of the batter onto the skillet for each pancake, spreading it out slightly with the back of a spoon to form a round shape. Cook the pancakes for 2-3 minutes on one side or until bubbles start to form on the surface and the edges look set.
- **Flip and cook:** Carefully flip the pancakes with a spatula and cook for an additional 1-2 minutes on the other side or until golden brown and cooked through.

Kotlety Mielone (Polish Meatballs)

PREP TIME: 15 MIN   COOKING TIME: 20 MIN   SERVES: 20   CALORIES PER SERVING: 150

Kotlety Mielone, or Polish Meatballs, are a beloved comfort food in Poland, often enjoyed as a hearty main dish served with mashed potatoes, noodles, or bread. These meatballs are typically made with a mixture of ground meat, onions, breadcrumbs, and seasonings, then pan-fried until golden and cooked through.

Ingredients

- 1 pound ground beef or pork
- 1 small onion, finely chopped
- 1/2 cup breadcrumbs
- 1 egg
- 2 cloves garlic, minced
- 1 teaspoon dried marjoram
- 1/2 teaspoon salt
- 1/4 teaspoon black pepper
- Vegetable oil for frying

Directions

- **Prepare the meatball mixture:** In a large mixing bowl, combine the ground beef or pork, finely chopped onion, breadcrumbs, egg, minced garlic, dried marjoram, salt, and black pepper. Use your hands to mix the ingredients together until well combined.

- **Form the meatballs:** Scoop out a small portion of the meatball mixture and roll it between your palms to form a smooth ball about 1-2 inches in diameter. Repeat with the remaining mixture until you have formed all the meatballs.

- **Pan-fry the meatballs:** Heat a few tablespoons of vegetable oil in a large skillet or frying pan over medium heat. Once the oil is hot, add the meatballs to the skillet in batches, making sure not to overcrowd the pan. Cook the meatballs for 4-5 minutes on each side or until they are golden brown and cooked through. You may need to adjust the heat to prevent them from burning. Drain and serve.

Jajka w Majonezie (Egg Salad)

PREP TIME: 10 MIN   COOKING TIME: 10 MIN   SERVES: 4   CALORIES PER SERVING: 200

Jajka W Majonezie, or Egg Salad, is a simple and versatile dish enjoyed as a sandwich filling, spread on crackers, or served on a bed of lettuce as a light meal. This classic Polish salad features hard-boiled eggs mixed with creamy mayonnaise, tangy mustard, and a touch of fresh herbs for added flavor. It's a popular choice for picnics, parties, and quick lunches, and it's easy to customize with your favorite ingredients.

Ingredients

You Need:

- 6 hard-boiled eggs, peeled and chopped
- 1/4 cup mayonnaise
- 1 tablespoon Dijon mustard
- 1 tablespoon chopped fresh parsley or chives
- 1/2 teaspoon paprika
- Salt and pepper to taste
- Optional: chopped celery, red onion, pickles, or capers for added flavor and texture

Directions

- **Prepare the hard-boiled eggs:** Place the eggs in a saucepan and cover them with cold water. Bring the water to a boil over medium-high heat, then reduce the heat to low and simmer for 8-10 minutes. Once cooked, remove the eggs from the water and let them cool before peeling and chopping them.

- **Make the egg salad:** In a large mixing bowl, combine the chopped hard-boiled eggs, mayonnaise, Dijon mustard, chopped fresh parsley or chives, and paprika. Stir the ingredients together until well combined. If desired, you can also add chopped celery, red onion, pickles, or capers for added flavor and texture.

- **Season to taste:** Taste the egg salad and season with salt and pepper to taste. Adjust the seasonings as needed to suit your preferences.

- **Chill the salad:** Cover the bowl with plastic wrap or a lid and refrigerate the egg salad for at least 30 minutes to allow the flavors to meld together.

Półmisek Zakąsek (Assorted Appetizers Platter)

PREP TIME: 20 MIN   COOKING TIME: 0 MIN   SERVES: 4-6   CALORIES PER SERVING: 200

Półmisek Zakąsek, or Assorted Appetizers Platter, is a traditional Polish dish often served as a starter or appetizer at family gatherings, parties, and celebrations. This colorful and flavorful platter features an assortment of cold cuts, cheeses, pickles, olives, bread, and other finger foods

Ingredients

You Need:
- Assorted cold cuts (such as ham, salami, and roast beef)
- Assorted cheeses (such as cheddar, Swiss, and gouda)
- Pickles (such as dill pickles, gherkins, and pickled onions)
- Olives (such as green and black olives)
- Cherry tomatoes
- Sliced cucumbers
- Sliced bell peppers (red, yellow, and green)
- Hard-boiled eggs, halved or sliced
- Crispbread or sliced baguette
- Mustard and/or mayonnaise for dipping
- Fresh herbs for garnish (such as parsley or dill)

Directions

- **Prepare the ingredients:** Arrange the assorted cold cuts, cheeses, pickles, olives, cherry tomatoes, sliced cucumbers, sliced bell peppers, and hard-boiled eggs on a large platter or serving tray. You can arrange them in individual piles or group them together for variety.

- **Add the bread:** Place crispbread or sliced baguette on the platter alongside the other ingredients. Toast the bread slices if you desire to add crunch.

- **Garnish and serve:** Garnish the platter with fresh herbs, such as parsley or dill, for a pop of color and flavor.

Pomidory Faszerowane (Stuffed Tomatoes)

PREP TIME: 20 MIN   COOKING TIME: 30 MIN   SERVES: 4-6   CALORIES PER SERVING: 200

Pomidory Faszerowane, or Stuffed Tomatoes, are a popular Polish dish enjoyed as a light appetizer or side dish. They make a delicious addition to any meal and are a great way to showcase the fresh flavors of summer tomatoes.

Ingredients

You Need:

- 6 large tomatoes
- 1/2 cup uncooked rice
- 1 cup water or broth
- 1 tablespoon vegetable oil
- 1 small onion, finely chopped
- 2 cloves garlic, minced
- 8 ounces ground meat (such as beef, pork, or chicken)
- 1/2 teaspoon salt
- 1/4 teaspoon black pepper
- 1 teaspoon dried herbs (such as thyme, oregano, or basil)
- 1/4 cup grated Parmesan cheese (optional)
- Fresh parsley or dill for garnish

Directions

- **Prepare the tomatoes:** Preheat your oven to 375°F (190°C). Slice the tops off the tomatoes and carefully scoop out the seeds and pulp using a spoon, leaving a hollow cavity.
- **Cook the rice:** In a small saucepan, combine the uncooked rice and water or broth. Bring the mixture to a boil over medium heat, then reduce the heat to low, cover, and simmer for 15-20 minutes. Remove the saucepan from the heat and let the rice cool slightly.
- **Prepare the filling:** In a large skillet or frying pan, heat the vegetable oil over medium heat. Add the chopped onion and minced garlic, and cook until softened and translucent, about 5 minutes. Add the ground meat to the skillet and cook, breaking it apart with a spoon, until browned and cooked through, about 8-10 minutes. Season the meat mixture with herbs and seasoning.
- **Combine the filling:** In a mixing bowl, combine the cooked rice and the meat mixture, stirring until well combined. Stir in the grated Parmesan cheese for extra flavor.
- **Stuff the tomatoes:** Spoon the rice and meat mixture into the hollowed-out tomatoes, pressing down gently to pack the filling inside. You can mound the filling on top of the tomatoes for a rustic look.
- **Bake the stuffed tomatoes:** Place the stuffed tomatoes in a baking dish or on a baking sheet lined with parchment paper. Bake in the preheated oven for 20-25 minutes, or until the tomatoes are tender and the filling is heated through and golden brown on top.

Kaszanka na Ciepło (Warm Blood Sausage)

PREP TIME: 20 MIN   **COOKING TIME: 30 MIN**   **SERVES: 4**   **CALORIES PER SERVING: 400**

Kaszanka na Ciepło, or Warm Blood Sausage, is a traditional Polish dish made from a mixture of cooked buckwheat groats, pork blood, and spices, stuffed into sausage casings and simmered until cooked through.

Ingredients
You Need:
- 1 cup buckwheat groats
- 2 cups water
- 1/2 pound pork blood (available at specialty butchers or online)
- 1/4 pound bacon, diced
- 1 small onion, finely chopped
- 2 cloves garlic, minced
- 1 teaspoon dried marjoram
- 1/2 teaspoon ground black pepper
- 1/4 teaspoon ground allspice
- Salt to taste
- Pork intestines or sausage casings (available at specialty butchers or online)
- Vegetable oil for frying
- Sautéed onions for serving (optional)
- Crusty bread or mashed potatoes for serving

Directions
- **Prepare the buckwheat groats:** Rinse the buckwheat groats under cold water and drain well. In a saucepan, bring 2 cups of water to a boil. Add the rinsed buckwheat groats to the boiling water, reduce the heat to low, cover, and simmer for 15-20 minutes. Remove the saucepan from the heat and let the cooked buckwheat groats cool slightly.
- **Cook the bacon and onions:** In a skillet or frying pan, cook the diced bacon over medium heat until it starts to render its fat and becomes crispy, about 5-7 minutes. Add the finely chopped onion to the skillet and cook, stirring occasionally, until the onion is soft and translucent, about 5 minutes. Add the minced garlic to the skillet and cook for an additional 1-2 minutes.
- **Prepare the sausage mixture:** In a large mixing bowl, combine the cooked buckwheat groats, cooked bacon and onion mixture, pork blood, dried marjoram, ground black pepper, ground allspice, and salt to taste. Stir the ingredients together until well combined.
- **Stuff the sausage casings:** Using a sausage stuffer or a funnel, carefully fill the casings with the sausage mixture, tying off the ends with kitchen twine to form individual sausages.
- **Cook the sausages:** In a large pot, bring water to a gentle simmer. Add the stuffed sausages to the pot and simmer them for 15-20 minutes or until they are cooked through and firm to the touch. Be careful not to boil the sausages, as this can cause them to burst.

Kanapki (Open-Faced Sandwiches)

PREP TIME: 15 MIN   COOKING TIME: 0 MIN   SERVES: 4-6   CALORIES PER SERVING: 250

Kanapki, or Open-Faced Sandwiches, are a popular Polish dish enjoyed as a light meal or snack. They are often served at parties, gatherings, and celebrations, as well as for breakfast or lunch. These sandwiches are versatile and customizable.

Ingredients

You Need:
- Sliced bread (such as rye, whole grain, or white)
- Butter or mayonnaise for spreading
- Toppings of your choice (see suggestions below)
- Fresh herbs or microgreens for garnish

Possible Toppings
- Sliced meats (such as ham, turkey, or roast beef)
- Sliced cheeses (such as cheddar, Swiss, or gouda)
- Hard-boiled eggs, sliced or mashed
- Smoked salmon or trout
- Cucumber slices
- Tomato slices
- Radish slices
- Avocado slices or mashed avocado

Directions

- **Prepare the bread:** Toast the slices of bread until golden brown and crisp, if desired. Alternatively, you can use untoasted bread for a softer texture.

- **Spread the butter or mayonnaise:** Spread a thin layer of butter or mayonnaise on each slice of bread. This will help the toppings adhere to the bread and add flavor and moisture.

- **Arrange the toppings:** Arrange the desired toppings on the prepared slices of bread, layering them evenly to create an attractive presentation. You can mix and match toppings to create a variety of flavor combinations.

- **Garnish:** Garnish the open-faced sandwiches with fresh herbs or microgreens for a pop of color and freshness. You can also sprinkle with salt and pepper or drizzle with olive oil or balsamic vinegar if desired.

Pierogi z Serem (Polish Cheese Pierogi)

PREP TIME: 1 HOUR COOKING TIME: 15 MIN   SERVINGS: 30 CALORIES PER SERVING: 150

Pierogi z Serem, or Polish Cheese Pierogi, are a beloved traditional dish in Poland. While pierogi are often associated with savory fillings like potatoes and meat, cheese pierogi offer a delightful twist with their creamy and indulgent cheese filling.

Ingredients

You Need:
For the Dough
- 2 cups all-purpose flour
- 1 large egg
- 1/2 cup sour cream
- 1/4 cup unsalted butter, melted
- 1/2 teaspoon salt

For the Cheese Filling
- 1 cup farmer's cheese or dry cottage cheese
- 1/2 cup cream cheese
- 1 large egg yolk
- 2 tablespoons granulated sugar
- 1/2 teaspoon vanilla extract
-
- For Serving
- Sour cream (optional)
- Fresh herbs such as chives or parsley (optional)

Directions

- **Prepare the Dough:** In a large mixing bowl, combine the flour and salt. Make a well in the center and add the egg, sour cream, and melted butter. Mix until the dough comes together. Turn the dough out onto a floured surface and knead for about 5 minutes or until smooth and elastic. Wrap the dough in plastic wrap and let it rest for 30 minutes.

- **Make the Cheese Filling:** In another mixing bowl, combine the farmer's cheese, cream cheese, egg yolk, sugar, and vanilla extract. Mix until smooth and well combined. Set aside.

- **Assemble the Pierogi:** Roll out the dough on a floured surface to a thickness of about 1/8 inch. Use a round cookie cutter or glass to cut out circles of dough. Place a small spoonful of the cheese filling in the center of each dough circle. Fold the dough over the filling to create a half-moon shape, then press the edges firmly to seal. You can use a fork to crimp the edges for a decorative touch.

- **Cook the Pierogi:** Bring a large pot of salted water to a boil. Carefully drop the pierogi into the boiling water, a few at a time, and cook for about 3-4 minutes or until they float to the surface. Using a slotted spoon, remove the cooked pierogi from the water and transfer them to a plate. Repeat until all the pierogi are cooked.

Chapter Four

Drinks (Napoje)

Kompot (Fruit Juice)

PREP TIME: 10 MIN   **COOKING TIME: 30 MIN**   **SERVES: 8**   **CALORIES PER SERVING: 60**

Kompot is a traditional Polish drink made from simmering fresh or dried fruits with sugar and spices. It is often served chilled during the summer and warm during the winter, making it a versatile beverage enjoyed year-round. Kompot is not only refreshing but also a great way to use up those leftover fruits.

Ingredients

You Need:

- 6 cups water
- 1 cup sugar (adjust to taste)
- 2 apples, cored and sliced
- 2 pears, cored and sliced
- 1 cup cherries, pitted (can use fresh or frozen)
- 1 cup strawberries, hulled and halved
- 1 lemon, sliced
- 1 cinnamon stick
- 2 cloves
- Fresh mint leaves for garnish (optional)

Directions

- **Prepare the fruit:** Wash and prepare all the fruit. Core and slice the apples and pears, pit the cherries, and hull and halve the strawberries.

- **Boil the water:** In a large pot, bring 6 cups of water to a boil. Add the ingredients.

- Add the sugar, apples, pears, cherries, strawberries, lemon slices, cinnamon sticks, and cloves to the boiling water. Stir to dissolve the sugar.

- **Simmer the kompot:** Reduce the heat to low and let the mixture simmer for about 30 minutes, or until the fruit is soft and the flavors have melded together.

- **Cool and strain (optional):** If you prefer a clear juice, you can strain the kompot to remove the fruit and spices. Otherwise, you can leave the fruit in the drink for added texture and flavor. Allow the kompot to cool to room temperature. Once cooled, transfer the kompot to a pitcher and refrigerate until thoroughly chilled.

Cytrynówka (Polish Lemon Vodka Liqueur)

PREP TIME: 15 MIN   COOKING TIME: NONE   SERVES: 25   CALORIES PER SERVING: 70

Cytrynówka is a traditional Polish lemon vodka liqueur often homemade and shared during gatherings and celebrations. It is known for its vibrant lemon flavor and can be enjoyed straight, on the rocks, or as a base for cocktails. This liqueur highlights the Polish tradition of crafting flavored vodkas.

Ingredients

You Need:
- 6 large lemons (preferably organic, since the zest is used)
- 2 cups granulated sugar
- 4 cups vodka (preferably a high-quality Polish vodka)
- 2 cups water

Directions

- **Prepare the lemons:** Wash the lemons thoroughly. Use a vegetable peeler or a zester to remove the zest from the lemons, avoiding the white pith as much as possible, as it can be bitter. Set the lemons aside to juice later.
- **Make the simple syrup:** In a medium saucepan, combine the sugar and water. Heat over medium heat, stirring occasionally, until the sugar is completely dissolved. Remove from heat and let the simple syrup cool to room temperature.
- **Combine ingredients:** In a large, clean glass jar or bottle with a tight-fitting lid, combine the lemon zest, lemon juice (from the lemons you zested), and vodka. Add the cooled simple syrup to the mixture. Stir or shake gently to combine.
- **Infuse the liqueur:** Seal the jar or bottle and store it in a cool, dark place. Let the mixture infuse for 1 to 2 weeks, shaking the jar gently every day to help the flavors meld.
- **Strain and bottle:** After the infusion period, strain the liqueur through a fine-mesh sieve or cheesecloth to remove the lemon zest and any solids. Pour the strained liqueur into clean bottles or jars and seal tightly.

Krówka (Caramel Drink)

PREP TIME: 10 MIN   COOKING TIME: 15 MIN   SERVES: 6   CALORIES PER SERVING: 250

"Krówka" means "baby cow" in Polish and refers to a popular type of soft caramel candy enjoyed in Poland. Inspired by these beloved candies, the Krówka drink captures their rich, creamy, and caramel flavor in liquid form, making it a delightful and nostalgic beverage for many Poles.

Ingredients

You Need:
- 1 cup granulated sugar
- 1/4 cup water
- 2 cups whole milk
- 1 cup heavy cream
- 1 teaspoon vanilla extract
- 1/4 teaspoon salt
- 1/4 cup vodka (optional, for an alcoholic version)

Directions

- **Prepare the caramel:** Combine the sugar and water in a medium saucepan. Heat over medium heat, stirring gently until the sugar dissolves. Once dissolved, stop stirring and let the mixture simmer until it turns a deep amber color, about 8-10 minutes. Be careful not to burn the caramel.

- **Add the dairy:** Carefully add the milk and heavy cream to the caramel. The mixture will bubble vigorously, so pour slowly and stir continuously. Continue to stir until the caramel is fully dissolved into the milk and cream.

- **Add flavoring:** Remove the saucepan from the heat and stir in the vanilla extract and salt. If you're making the alcoholic version, add the vodka at this stage and mix well.

- **Cool the drink:** Allow the caramel drink to cool to room temperature. If you prefer a cold drink, you can serve it warm or transfer it to the refrigerator to chill.

Miód Pitny (Polish Honey Drink)

PREP TIME: 30 MIN   COOKING TIME: 1HOUR   SERVES: 25   CALORIES PER SERVING: 150

Miód Pitny, or Polish Honey Drink, is one of the oldest alcoholic beverages in the world, with a history dating back to ancient times. It was highly valued in medieval Poland and often used in royal courts and ceremonies. The name "miód pitny" literally translates to "drinkable honey," reflecting its primary ingredient.

Ingredients

You Need:

- 2.5 kg (5.5 lbs) honey
- 7.5 liters (2 gallons) water
- 2 lemons (juiced)
- 2 oranges (juiced)
- 1 teaspoon whole cloves
- 2 cinnamon sticks
- 1 teaspoon whole allspice berries
- 1 packet of mead yeast (or wine yeast)
- 1 teaspoon yeast nutrient (optional, but recommended)

Directions

- **Prepare the honey:** Combine the honey and water in a large pot. Heat the mixture over medium heat, stirring frequently, until the honey is fully dissolved. Do not let it boil.
- **Add spices and citrus:** Once the honey is dissolved, add the lemon juice, orange juice, cloves, cinnamon sticks, and allspice berries to the pot. Allow the mixture to simmer gently for about 30 minutes, stirring occasionally.
- **Cool the mixture:** Remove the pot from heat and let the mixture cool to room temperature. This can take a few hours. Speed up the process by placing the pot in a sink filled with cold water, stirring occasionally. While the must is cooling, rehydrate the yeast according to the instructions on the packet. If using yeast nutrient, add it to the yeast mixture.
- **Fermentation:** Once the honey has cooled to room temperature, transfer it to a sanitized fermentation vessel. Add the prepared yeast to the must and stir well to combine.
- **Primary fermentation:** Seal the fermentation vessel with an airlock and store it in a dark, cool place (around 18-22°C or 64-72°F). Allow the mead to ferment for 1 to 2 months; after primary fermentation is complete, transfer (rack) the mead to a secondary fermentation vessel, leaving behind any sediment. Seal with an airlock and allow the mead to age for at least 4 to 6 months. Once the mead has aged to your satisfaction, transfer it to sanitized bottles and seal them tightly. Store the bottles in a cool, dark place. The mead will continue to improve with age and can be stored for several years.

Piwo z Miodem (Beer with Honey)

PREP TIME: 5 MIN   **COOKING TIME: 5 MIN**   **SERVES: 1**   **CALORIES PER SERVING: 100**

Piwo z Miodem, or beer with honey, is a traditional Polish drink that combines the bitterness of beer with the sweetness of honey. This combination has been enjoyed for centuries, especially during the colder months, as the honey adds a warming and soothing element to the beverage.

Ingredients

You Need:

- 1 bottle (500 ml) of lager or pale ale (a Polish beer like Żywiec or Tyskie works well)
- 1-2 tablespoons of honey (to taste)
- 1 cinnamon stick (optional)
- 1-2 slices of lemon (optional)

Directions

- **Warm the beer:** Pour the beer into a small saucepan and gently warm it over low heat. Do not let it boil, as boiling will cause the alcohol to evaporate and alter the flavor of the beer.

- **Add the honey:** Once the beer is warm, remove the saucepan from the heat. Stir in the honey until it is fully dissolved. Start with 1 tablespoon of honey and add more if you prefer a sweeter taste.

- **Optional additions:** For a spiced version, add a cinnamon stick to the saucepan while warming the beer. You can also add lemon slices for a citrusy twist.

Herbata z Prątnic (Herbal Tea)

PREP TIME: 5 MIN   **COOKING TIME: 10 MIN**   **SERVES: 4**   **CALORIES PER SERVING: 5**

Herbata z Prątnic, also known as Polish herbal tea, often includes various herbs traditionally used in Polish folk medicine for their soothing and healing properties. Prątnic refers to the common use of various plants and herbs, making it a unique and personalized drink based on available ingredients and individual preferences.

Ingredients

You Need:

- 1 tablespoon dried chamomile flowers
- 1 tablespoon dried mint leaves
- 1 tablespoon dried lemon balm leaves
- 1 tablespoon dried linden flowers
- 1 teaspoon dried nettle leaves
- 1 liter (4 cups) water
- Honey (optional, to taste)
- Lemon slices (optional, for serving)

Directions

- **Prepare the herbs:** Measure out the dried herbs and combine them in a bowl. Adjust the quantities or add other herbs based on your preferences.

- **Boil the water:** In a kettle or pot, bring 1 liter of water to a boil.

- **Steep the herbs:** Place the combined dried herbs into a teapot or a heat-proof container. Pour the boiling water over the herbs.

- **Cover and steep:** Cover the teapot or container with a lid and let the herbs steep for about 10 minutes. This allows the herbs' flavors and beneficial properties to infuse into the water.

- **Strain the tea:** After steeping, strain the tea to remove the herbs. You can use a fine-mesh strainer or a cheesecloth for this purpose.

- **Add honey and lemon (optional):** If desired, add honey to sweeten the tea. Stir well until the honey is dissolved. You can also add lemon slices for an extra burst of flavor.

Oranżada (Orange Soda)

PREP TIME: 10 MIN **COOKING TIME: NONE** **SERVES: 4** **CALORIES PER SERVING: 120**

Oranżada, a nostalgic beverage for many Poles, dates back to the 19th century. It was initially made by pharmacists who mixed orange syrup with carbonated water, creating a refreshing and sweet fizzy drink. Today, it remains a popular and cherished treat, especially during summer.

Ingredients

You Need:

- 1 cup freshly squeezed orange juice (about 4 oranges)
- 1 tablespoon lemon juice
- 1/2 cup simple syrup (adjust to taste)
- 1 liter (4 cups) carbonated water (club soda)
- Ice cubes
- Orange slices, for garnish (optional)
- Mint leaves, for garnish (optional)

Directions

- **Prepare the simple syrup:** If you don't have simple syrup ready, you can make it by dissolving equal parts sugar and water in a saucepan over low heat. Stir until the sugar is completely dissolved, then let it cool.

- **Mix the juices and syrup:** In a large pitcher, combine the freshly squeezed orange juice, lemon juice, and simple syrup. Adjust the amount of syrup based on your desired sweetness.

- **Add the carbonated water:** Slowly pour in the carbonated water (club soda) and stir gently to mix. Be careful not to stir too vigorously to keep the carbonation. Serve with ice.

Kwas Chlebowy (Fermented Bread Drink)

PREP TIME: 30 MIN   COOKING TIME: 10 MIN   SERVES: 8   CALORIES PER SERVING: 150

Kwas Chlebowy, also known as Kvass in some regions, is a traditional Slavic beverage with a history dating back over a thousand years. It is made from fermented rye bread and was historically consumed by peasants as a low-alcoholic drink. Known for its distinctive tangy flavor, it is often considered a natural probiotic and a refreshing summer beverage.

Ingredients

You Need:

- 500 grams (1 lb) rye bread, preferably stale and cut into cubes
- 4 liters (1 gallon) water
- 200 grams (1 cup) sugar
- 10 grams (1 tablespoon) active dry yeast
- Handful of raisins (optional)
- Fresh mint leaves (optional, for garnish)

Directions

- **Toast the bread:** Preheat your oven to 180°C (350°F). Spread the rye bread cubes on a baking sheet and toast in the oven until they are dark brown but not burnt, about 10-15 minutes. This will give the drink its characteristic flavor.
- **Boil the water:** In a large pot, bring the water to a boil. Remove from heat.
- **Soak the bread:** Add the toasted bread cubes to the hot water. Cover and let it steep for about 4-5 hours or until the water has cooled to room temperature.
- **Strain the mixture:** Once the mixture has cooled, strain the liquid through a fine-mesh sieve or cheesecloth into a large, clean container. Discard the bread solids.
- **Add sugar and yeast:** Stir in the sugar until it dissolves completely. Add the yeast.
- **Fermentation:** Cover the container with a clean cloth and let it sit at room temperature for 2-3 days. The drink should start to ferment and develop a slightly fizzy texture. You can taste it periodically to achieve your desired level of fermentation.
- **Bottle the kwass:** Once fermented to your liking, strain the liquid again and pour it into clean bottles, leaving some space at the top. If desired, add a few raisins to each bottle for additional natural carbonation.
- **Refrigerate:** Seal the bottles tightly and refrigerate for another 24 hours. This will slow down the fermentation process and chill the drink.

Sirop Malinowy (Raspberry Syrup)

PREP TIME: 10 MIN COOKING TIME: 10 MIN   SERVES: 2   CALORIES PER SERVING: 60

Raspberry syrup, known as "Sirop Malinowy" in Polish, is a versatile and delicious syrup used in a variety of beverages and desserts. It captures the sweet and tart flavors of raspberries, making it a delightful addition to cocktails, lemonades, teas, and desserts.

Ingredients

You Need:
- 3 cups fresh raspberries
- 1 cup water
- 1 cup granulated sugar
- 1 tablespoon lemon juice

Directions

- **Prepare the raspberries:** Rinse the fresh raspberries under cold water and drain them thoroughly.

- **Cook the raspberries:** In a saucepan, combine the raspberries and water. Bring the mixture to a simmer over medium heat, stirring occasionally. Let it simmer for about 5 minutes until the raspberries have softened and released their juices.

- **Strain the mixture:** Once the raspberries have softened, pour the mixture through a fine-mesh sieve or cheesecloth into a clean bowl. Use a spoon to press the raspberries against the sieve to extract as much liquid as possible. Discard the solids.

- **Add sugar and lemon juice:** Return the strained raspberry liquid to the saucepan. Stir in the granulated sugar and lemon juice. Bring the mixture to a gentle boil over medium heat, stirring constantly until the sugar has completely dissolved. Reduce the heat to low and let the syrup simmer for another 5 minutes, allowing it to thicken slightly.

- **Cool and store:** Remove the saucepan from the heat and let the raspberry syrup cool to room temperature. Once cooled, transfer the syrup to a clean glass jar or bottle with a tight-fitting lid.

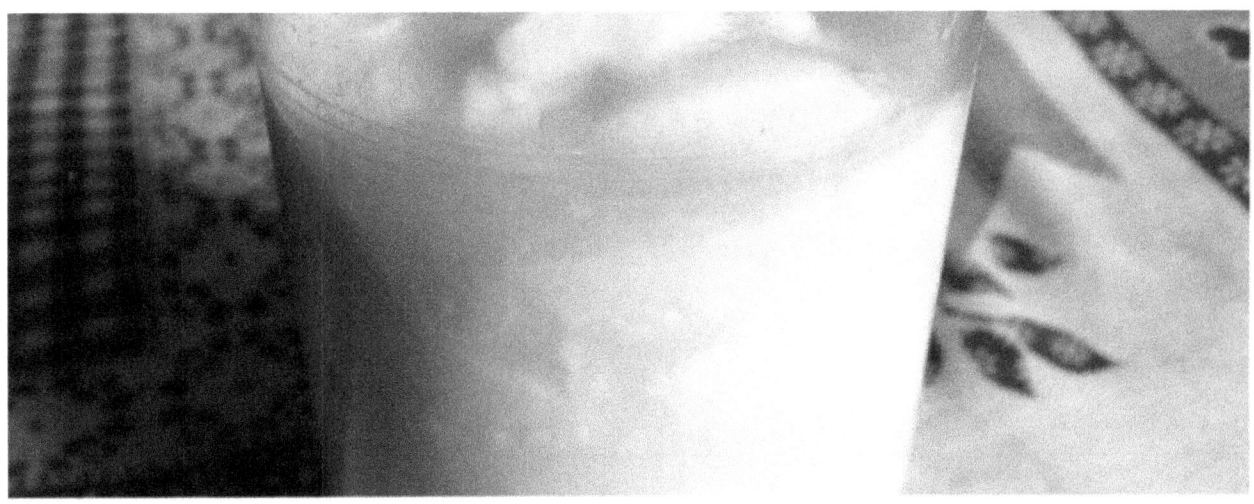

Zsiadłe Mleko (Soured Milk)

PREP TIME: 5 MIN   COOKING TIME: 0 MIN   SERVES: 4   CALORIES PER SERVING: 80

Zsiadłe Mleko, which translates to "soured milk or Kefir" in Polish, is a traditional drink in Poland and other Eastern European countries. It's often consumed as a refreshing beverage, particularly during hot summer days.

Ingredients

You Need:
- 4 cups buttermilk
- 2 tablespoons sugar (adjust to taste)
- 1/2 teaspoon vanilla extract (optional)
- Fresh berries or mint leaves for garnish (optional)

Directions

- Combine the buttermilk, sugar, and vanilla extract (if using) in a large pitcher. Stir until the sugar is dissolved.
- Taste the mixture and adjust the sweetness if necessary by adding more sugar.
- Chill the Zsiadłe Mleko in the refrigerator for at least 30 minutes before serving.
- Once chilled, pour the Zsiadłe Mleko into glasses and garnish with fresh berries or mint leaves if desired.
- Serve cold.

Chapter Five

Desserts (Deserty)

Pączki (Polish Donuts)

PREP TIME: 20 MIN   COOKING TIME: 30 MIN   SERVES: 20   CALORIES PER SERVING: 250

Pączki (pronounced "pohnch-kee") are traditional Polish donuts typically enjoyed on Fat Thursday (Tłusty Czwartek), which is the Thursday before Ash Wednesday. This day marks the beginning of Lent, and paczki were originally made to use up all the lard, sugar, eggs, and fruit in the house, as these items were forbidden during Lent.

Ingredients

You Need:
Dough
- 2 1/4 teaspoons (1 packet) active dry yeast
- 1/4 cup warm water (110°F/45°C)
- 1/2 cup granulated sugar
- 3/4 cup whole milk, warmed
- 4 cups all-purpose flour, plus more for dusting
- 1/2 teaspoon salt
- 4 large egg yolks
- 1 large egg
- 1/4 cup unsalted butter, melted
- 1 teaspoon vanilla extract
- 1 teaspoon rum (optional, for flavor)
- Zest of 1 lemon
- **Filling**
- 1 cup fruit preserves (e.g., raspberry, apricot, or prune)
- **For Frying**
- 1 quart vegetable oil (for deep frying)

Directions

- **Prepare the Yeast Mixture:** Dissolve the yeast in the warm water along with a teaspoon of the granulated sugar. Let it sit for about 10 minutes until it becomes foamy.
- **Make the Dough:** In a large mixing bowl, combine the remaining granulated sugar, warm milk, and yeast mixture. Add 2 cups of flour and mix until smooth. Beat in the egg yolks, whole egg, melted butter, vanilla extract, rum (if using), and lemon zest. Gradually add the remaining flour and salt, mixing until a soft dough forms.
- **Knead the Dough:** Turn the dough onto a floured surface and knead for about 8-10 minutes until smooth and elastic. Place the dough in a lightly oiled bowl, cover it with a clean towel, and let it rise in a warm place for about 1 to 1 1/2 hours or until doubled in size.
- **Shape the Paczki:** Punch down the dough and turn it out onto a floured surface. Roll it out to about 1/2-inch thickness. Use a round cutter (about 3 inches in diameter) to cut out circles of dough. Place a teaspoon of fruit preserves in the center of each circle, fold the dough over the filling, and pinch the edges to seal. Shape into a ball and place on a floured surface. Cover with a towel and let rise for another 30 minutes.
- **Fry the Paczki:** Heat the vegetable oil in a deep fryer or large, heavy pot to 350°F (175°C). Fry the paczki in batches, about 2-3 minutes on each side, until golden brown. Use a slotted spoon to remove the paczki and drain them on paper towels.

Toping:

- Sprinkle icing sugar and enjoy!

Sernik (Polish Cheesecake)

PREP TIME: 30 MIN COOKING TIME: 1 HR 15   SERVES: 12   CALORIES PER SERVING: 320

Sernik, a beloved dessert in Poland, has roots dating back to the 17th century. It is traditionally made with twaróg, a type of fresh Polish cheese similar to farmer's cheese or quark. Sernik is often enjoyed during festive occasions, including Christmas and Easter, and each family has its own cherished version of the recipe.

Ingredients

You Need:

Crust
- 1 1/2 cups racker crumbs
- 1/4 cup granulated sugar
- 1/2 cup unsalted butter

Filling
- 2 pounds twaróg cheese (or ricotta cheese if twaróg is unavailable)
- 1 cup granulated sugar
- 1/2 cup sour cream
- 4 large eggs
- 1 teaspoon vanilla extract
- 1/2 teaspoon almond extract
- 2 tablespoons all-purpose flour
- Zest of 1 lemon

Topping (optional)
- 1 cup sour cream
- 2 tablespoons powdered sugar
- 1/2 teaspoon vanilla extract

Directions

- **Prepare the Crust:** Preheat your oven to 350°F (175°C). In a medium bowl, combine the graham cracker crumbs, granulated sugar, and melted butter. Mix until the crumbs are evenly moistened. Press the mixture firmly into the bottom of a 9-inch springform pan. Use the back of a spoon or a flat-bottomed glass to press it evenly. Bake the crust for 10 minutes, then remove from the oven and set aside to cool.
- **Prepare the Filling:** In a large mixing bowl, beat the twaróg cheese until smooth. If using ricotta, strain it first to remove excess moisture. Add the granulated sugar and mix until well combined. Add the sour cream, eggs, vanilla extract, almond extract (if using), flour, and lemon zest. Mix until smooth and creamy.
- **Bake the Cheesecake:** Pour the cheese mixture over the cooled crust, spreading it evenly. Place the springform pan in a larger baking dish. Fill the larger dish with hot water until it reaches halfway up the sides of the springform pan (this water bath helps to prevent cracks in the cheesecake). Bake for about 1 hour 15 minutes, or until the center is set and the top is lightly golden.
- **Cool the Cheesecake:** Turn off the oven and crack the door open. Let the cheesecake cool in the oven for 1 hour to prevent cracking. Remove the cheesecake from the oven and water bath. Run a knife around the edge of the pan to loosen the cheesecake and allow it to cool completely at room temperature. Refrigerate for at least 4 hours or overnight for the best texture. Add toppings.

Makowiec (Poppy Seed Roll) Recipe

PREP TIME: 2 HOUR   COOKING TIME: 45 MIN   SERVES: 16   CALORIES PER SERVING: 300

Makowiec (pronounced "mah-KOH-vyets") is a traditional Polish dessert popular during Christmas and Easter. The poppy seed filling is believed to symbolize prosperity and fertility making this roll not just a treat but also a wish for good fortune in the coming year.

Ingredients

You Need:
Dough

- 2 1/4 teaspoons (1 packet) active dry yeast
- 1/4 cup warm water (110°F/45°C)
- 3/4 cup whole milk, warmed
- 1/4 cup granulated sugar
- 4 cups all-purpose flour, plus more for dusting
- 1/2 teaspoon salt
- 1/4 cup unsalted butter, melted
- 3 large egg yolks
- 1 teaspoon vanilla extract

Poppy Seed Filling

- 2 cups poppy seeds
- 1 cup whole milk
- 1/2 cup granulated sugar
- 1/4 cup honey
- 1/4 cup unsalted butter
- 1 teaspoon vanilla extract
- 1/2 teaspoon almond extract (optional)
- 1/2 cup raisins
- 1/2 cup chopped walnuts or almonds
- Zest of 1 lemon

Egg Wash

- 1 large egg, beaten with 1 tablespoon water

Glaze (optional)

- 1 cup powdered sugar
- 2-3 tablespoons lemon juice

Directions

- **Prepare the Dough:** Dissolve the yeast in the warm water with a pinch of sugar. Let it sit for about 10 minutes until it becomes foamy. In a large mixing bowl, combine the remaining sugar, warm milk, and yeast mixture. Add 2 cups of flour and mix until smooth. Beat in the egg yolks, melted butter, and vanilla extract. Gradually add the remaining flour and salt, mixing until a soft dough forms. Turn the dough onto a floured surface and knead for about 8-10 minutes until smooth and elastic. Place the dough in a lightly oiled bowl, cover it with a clean towel, and let it rise in a warm place for about 1 to 1 1/2 hours or until doubled in size.
- **Prepare the Poppy Seed Filling:** While the dough is rising, prepare the filling. In a saucepan, combine the poppy seeds and milk. Simmer over low heat for about 30 minutes, stirring occasionally, until the poppy seeds are tender and the milk is absorbed. Drain the poppy seed mixture if necessary and grind the seeds using a food processor or a grinder. In a large bowl, combine the ground poppy seeds, sugar, honey, butter, vanilla extract, almond extract (if using), raisins, chopped nuts, and lemon zest. Mix well to combine.
- **Assemble the Makowiec:** Preheat your oven to 350°F (175°C). Line a baking sheet with parchment paper. Punch down the risen dough and turn it out onto a floured surface. Roll it into a large rectangle, about 1/4-inch thick. Spread the poppy seed filling evenly over the dough, leaving a small border around the edges. Starting from one of the long sides, roll the dough tightly into a log. Pinch the seams and ends to seal. Place the roll seam-side down on the prepared baking sheet. Cover with a towel and let it rise for 30 minutes.
- **Bake the Makowiec:** Brush the top of the roll with the beaten egg wash. Bake for about 40-45 minutes or until golden brown and cooked through. Let the roll cool on a wire rack.
- **Prepare the Glaze (Optional):** In a small bowl, mix the powdered sugar with enough lemon juice to make a smooth, pourable glaze. Drizzle the glaze over the cooled makowiec.

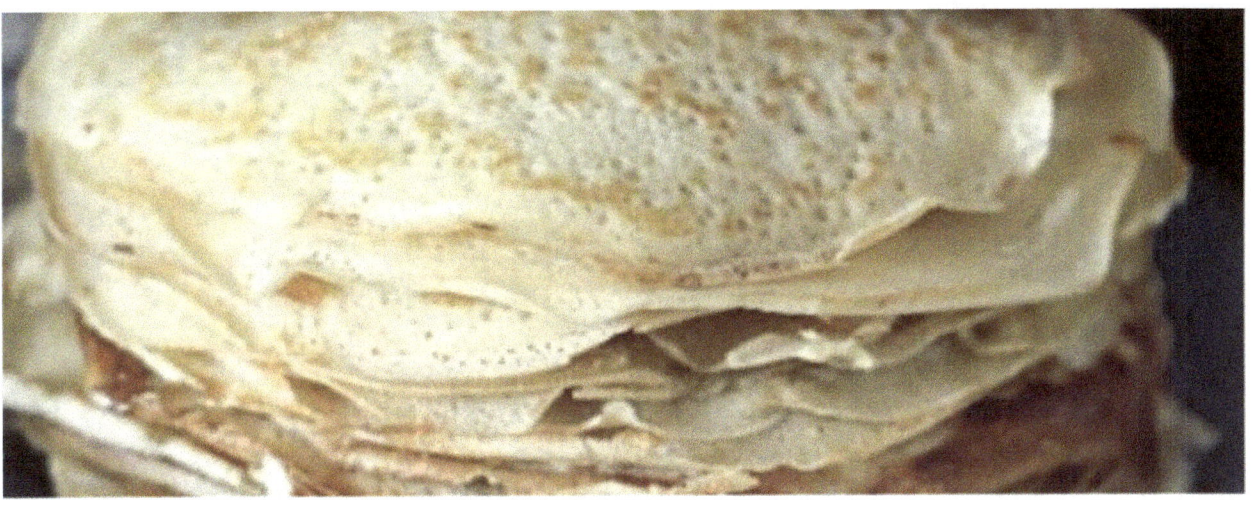

Naleśniki (Polish Crepes)

PREP TIME: 15 MIN **COOKING TIME: 30 MIN** **SERVES: 8** **CALORIES PER SERVING: 150**

Naleśniki (pronounced "nah-lesh-NEE-kee") are versatile Polish crepes that can be enjoyed with sweet or savory fillings. They are a popular dish for both breakfast and dessert in Poland. Similar to French crepes, naleśniki can be filled with a variety of ingredients, including sweet cheese, fruit, or savory mushrooms and cheese.

Ingredients

You Need:

Crepe Batter
- 1 cup all-purpose flour
- 1 1/4 cups whole milk
- 2 large eggs
- 1 tablespoon granulated sugar
- 1/4 teaspoon salt
- 2 tablespoons unsalted butter, melted
- 1 teaspoon vanilla extract (optional for sweet crepes)
- Extra butter or oil for cooking

Suggested Sweet Fillings
- Sweet cheese filling (twaróg mixed with sugar and vanilla)
- Fresh berries

Suggested Savory Fillings
- Sautéed mushrooms and cheese
- Spinach and feta

Directions

- **Prepare the Batter:** In a mixing bowl, whisk together the flour, milk, eggs, sugar, salt, melted butter, and vanilla extract (if using) until smooth and well combined. You can also use a blender for the smoothest batter. Let the batter rest for about 15 minutes to allow the flour to hydrate fully.

- **Cook the Crepes:** Heat a non-stick skillet or crepe pan over medium heat. Lightly grease the pan with a small amount of butter or oil. Pour about 1/4 cup of batter into the pan and immediately tilt the pan to spread the batter evenly into a thin layer. Cook for about 1-2 minutes, or until the edges start to lift and the bottom is lightly golden brown. Flip the crepe and cook for another 30 seconds to 1 minute, until the second side is lightly browned. Transfer the cooked crepe to a plate and repeat with the remaining batter, greasing the pan as needed.

- **Fill the Crepes:** Place your desired filling in the center of each crepe. For sweet fillings, spread ingredients like sweet cheese, Nutella, or jam. For savory fillings, add ingredients like sautéed mushrooms, cheese, or ham. Fold the crepes over the filling. You can fold them into quarters, roll them up, or fold them in half, depending on your preference.

Szarlotka (Polish Apple Cake)

PREP TIME: 30 MIN **COOKING TIME: 50 MIN** **SERVES: 12** **CALORIES PER SERVING: 300**

Szarlotka is a beloved Polish apple cake that holds a special place in Polish cuisine. It is often enjoyed with a dollop of whipped cream or a scoop of vanilla ice cream. This dessert is particularly popular in autumn when apples are in season, and it showcases the wonderful flavor of tart, juicy apples combined with a buttery, crumbly crust.

Ingredients
You Need:

Dough
- 2 1/2 cups all-purpose flour
- 1/2 cup granulated sugar
- 1/2 teaspoon salt
- 1 teaspoon baking powder
- 1 cup unsalted butter, cold and cut into small pieces
- 2 large eggs
- 1 teaspoon vanilla extract

Apple Filling
- 6 large apples (Granny Smith or other tart apples), peeled, cored, and sliced thinly
- 1/2 cup granulated sugar
- 1 teaspoon ground cinnamon
- 1 tablespoon lemon juice
- 1 tablespoon cornstarch

Topping
- Powdered sugar, for dusting

Directions

- **Prepare the Dough:** In a large mixing bowl, combine the flour, granulated sugar, salt, and baking powder. Cut in the cold butter using a pastry blender or your fingers until the mixture resembles coarse crumbs. Add the eggs and vanilla extract and mix until the dough comes together. If the dough is too dry, add a tablespoon of cold water at a time until it holds together. Divide the dough into two equal parts, wrap them in plastic wrap, and refrigerate for at least 30 minutes.
- **Prepare the Apple Filling:** In a large bowl, combine the sliced apples, granulated sugar, ground cinnamon, lemon juice, and cornstarch. Mix well to coat the apples evenly.
- **Assemble the Cake:** Preheat your oven to 350°F (175°C). Grease and flour a 9x13-inch baking dish. Roll out one portion of the dough on a floured surface to fit the bottom and sides of the baking dish. Transfer the dough to the prepared dish, pressing it into the corners and up the sides. Spread the apple filling evenly over the dough. Roll out the second portion of the dough to fit the top of the baking dish. Place it over the apple filling, pressing the edges to seal. You can also cut the dough into strips and create a lattice pattern on top if you prefer. Cut a few small slits in the top crust to allow steam to escape.
- **Bake the Szarlotka:** Bake in the preheated oven for 45-50 minutes.

Kremówka (Cream Cake)

PREP TIME: 45 MIN   **COOKING TIME: 30 MIN**   **SERVES: 12**   **CALORIES PER SERVING: 350**

Kremówka, also known as Napoleonka, is a beloved Polish dessert that gained fame when Pope John Paul II mentioned it as one of his favorite childhood treats from Wadowice, his hometown. This dessert features layers of flaky puff pastry filled with a rich, creamy custard.

Ingredients

You Need:

Pastry
- 2 sheets of puff pastry, thawed if frozen

Custard Filling
- 2 cups whole milk
- 1/2 cup granulated sugar
- 1 vanilla bean (or 2 teaspoons vanilla extract)
- 4 large egg yolks
- 1/4 cup cornstarch
- 2 tablespoons unsalted butter

Topping
- Powdered sugar, for dusting

Directions

- **Prepare the Pastry:** Preheat your oven to 400°F (200°C). Line two baking sheets with parchment paper. Roll out each puff pastry sheet to fit the baking sheets. Prick the pastry all over with a fork to prevent it from puffing up too much. Place the puff pastry sheets on the prepared baking sheets and bake for 10-15 minutes or until golden brown and crispy. If they puff up too much during baking, you can gently press them down with a spatula. Remove from the oven and let cool completely on a wire rack.
- **Prepare the Custard Filling:** In a medium saucepan, heat the milk over medium heat. If using a vanilla bean, split it lengthwise, scrape out the seeds, and add both the seeds and the pod to the milk. If using vanilla extract, add it later. In a bowl, whisk together the granulated sugar, egg yolks, and cornstarch until smooth and pale. Once the milk is hot (but not boiling), remove the vanilla pod (if used) and slowly pour the milk into the egg mixture, whisking constantly to temper the eggs. Pour the mixture back into the saucepan and cook over medium heat, stirring constantly, until the custard thickens and comes to a boil. Remove from heat and stir in the butter and vanilla extract (if not using a vanilla bean). Pour the custard into a bowl, cover it with plastic wrap touching the surface to prevent skin from forming, and let it cool to room temperature. Then refrigerate.
- **Assemble the Kremówka:** Once the puff pastry and custard are completely cooled, place one sheet of puff pastry on a serving platter. Spread the custard evenly over the pastry sheet. Place the second sheet of puff pastry on top of the custard, pressing down gently to ensure it adheres.
- **Chill the Cake:** Refrigerate the assembled kremówka for at least 1 hour to set.

Pączki z Marmoladą (Jam-Filled Doughnuts)

PREP TIME: 2 HOURS   COOKING TIME: 30 MIN   SERVES: 20   CALORIES PER SERVING: 300

Pączki (pronounced "pohnch-kee") are traditional Polish doughnuts typically enjoyed on Fat Thursday (Tłusty Czwartek) or Fat Tuesday (Mardi Gras), right before the start of Lent. This indulgence is meant to use up rich ingredients like butter, sugar, and eggs, which were traditionally avoided during Lent.

Ingredients

You Need:

Dough
- 2 1/4 teaspoons (1 packet) active dry yeast
- 1/4 cup warm water (110°F/45°C)
- 1/2 cup granulated sugar
- 3/4 cup whole milk, warmed
- 4 cups all-purpose flour, plus more for dusting
- 1/2 teaspoon salt
- 4 large egg yolks
- 1 large egg
- 1/4 cup unsalted butter, melted
- 1 teaspoon vanilla extract
- 1 teaspoon rum (optional, for flavor)
- Zest of 1 lemon

Filling
- 1 cup fruit preserves

For Frying
- 1 quart vegetable oil (for deep frying)

Topping
- 1 cup powdered sugar
- 1 teaspoon cinnamon (optional)

Directions

- **Prepare the Yeast Mixture:** Dissolve the yeast in the warm water along with a teaspoon of the granulated sugar. Let it sit for about 10 minutes until it becomes foamy.
- **Make the Dough:** In a large mixing bowl, combine the remaining granulated sugar, warm milk, and yeast mixture. Add 2 cups of flour and mix until smooth. Beat in the egg yolks, whole egg, melted butter, vanilla extract, rum (if using), and lemon zest. Gradually add the remaining flour and salt, mixing until a soft dough forms.
- **Knead the Dough:** Turn the dough onto a floured surface and knead for about 8-10 minutes until the dough is smooth and elastic. Place the dough in a lightly oiled bowl, cover it with a clean towel, and let it rise in a warm place for about 1 to 1 1/2 hours or until doubled in size.
- **Shape the Pączki:** Punch down the dough and turn it out onto a floured surface. Roll it out to about 1/2-inch thickness. Use a round cutter (about 3 inches in diameter) to cut out circles of dough. Place a teaspoon of fruit preserves in the center of each circle, fold the dough over the filling, and pinch the edges to seal. Shape into a ball and place on a floured surface. Cover with a towel and let rise for another 30 minutes.
- **Fry the Pączki:** Heat the vegetable oil in a deep fryer or large, heavy pot to 350°F (175°C). Fry the pączki in batches, about 2-3 minutes on each side, until golden brown. Use a slotted spoon to remove the pączki and drain them on paper towels. Rollin powdered sugar while warm.

Ptasie Mleczko (Bird's Milk Cake)

PREP TIME: 45 MIN   COOKING TIME: 10 MIN   SERVES: 16   CALORIES PER SERVING: 250

Ptasie Mleczko, which translates to "Bird's Milk," is a popular Polish dessert that features a light and airy mousse filling encased in a layer of chocolate. The name is a whimsical expression meaning something extremely rare and delightful, akin to "a rare delicacy."

Ingredients

You Need:

Chocolate Layer
- 1 cup semi-sweet chocolate chips
- 2 tablespoons unsalted butter

Mousse Filling
- 1 cup whole milk
- 3 tablespoons granulated sugar
- 1 tablespoon vanilla extract
- 1 packet (2 1/4 teaspoons) unflavored gelatin
- 1/4 cup cold water
- 1 cup heavy whipping cream

Directions

- **Prepare the Chocolate Layer:** Melt the chocolate chips and butter together in a double boiler or a heatproof bowl set over a pot of simmering water. Stir until smooth. Pour half of the melted chocolate into a greased 9x9-inch square baking dish, spreading it evenly to cover the bottom. Place the dish in the refrigerator to set while you prepare the mousse filling.
- **Prepare the Mousse Filling:** In a small bowl, sprinkle the gelatin over the cold water and let it bloom for about 5 minutes. In a medium saucepan, heat the milk and sugar over medium heat until the sugar is dissolved and the mixture is hot but not boiling. Remove the saucepan from heat and stir in the bloomed gelatin until fully dissolved. Let the mixture cool to room temperature. Stir in the vanilla extract. In a separate bowl, whip the heavy cream until stiff peaks form. Gently fold the whipped cream into the cooled milk mixture until well combined and smooth.
- **Assemble the Ptasie Mleczko:** Spread the mousse filling evenly over the set chocolate layer in the baking dish. Place the dish in the refrigerator and chill for about 1 hour or until the mousse is firm.
- **Top with Chocolate:** Once the mousse is set, reheat the remaining melted chocolate if necessary to make it pourable. Pour the melted chocolate over the mousse layer, spreading it evenly to cover. Return the dish to the refrigerator and chill for an additional 30 minutes or until the top chocolate layer is firm.

Kluski Śląskie (Silesian Dumplings)

PREP TIME: 30 MIN **COOKING TIME: 20 MIN** **SERVES: 4** **CALORIES PER SERVING: 200**

Kluski Śląskie, or Silesian dumplings, are a traditional dish from the Silesia region of Poland. These dumplings are characterized by their round shape with an indentation in the center, which is perfect for holding gravy or sauce. They are typically served as a side dish with meats and stews.

Ingredients

You Need:

- 2 pounds (about 1 kg) potatoes
- 1 large egg
- 1 cup potato flour (you may need a bit more or less depending on the consistency)
- Salt, to taste

Directions

- **Prepare the Potatoes:** Peel the potatoes and cut them into even-sized pieces. Place the potatoes in a large pot, cover with cold water, add a pinch of salt, and bring to a boil. Cook the potatoes until tender, about 15-20 minutes.
- **Mash the Potatoes:** Drain the cooked potatoes and let them cool slightly. Pass the potatoes through a potato ricer or mash them until very smooth. Avoid using a blender or food processor as it can make the potatoes gummy. Let the mashed potatoes cool completely.
- **Make the Dough:** Once the potatoes are cool, place them in a mixing bowl. Add the egg and mix well. Gradually add the potato flour, mixing until a smooth, pliable dough forms. The dough should not be sticky; if it is, add a bit more potato flour.
- **Shape the Dumplings:** Divide the dough into small portions and roll each portion into a ball about the size of a golf ball. Using your thumb, press an indentation into the center of each dumpling.
- **Cook the Dumplings:** Bring a large pot of salted water to a gentle boil. Carefully drop the dumplings into the boiling water in batches, being careful not to overcrowd the pot. Cook the dumplings until they float to the surface, then let them cook for an additional 2-3 minutes. Remove the dumplings with a slotted spoon and transfer to a serving dish.

Kluski na Parze (Steamed Dumplings)

PREP TIME: 1 HOUR   COOKING TIME: 20 MIN   SERVES: 8   CALORIES PER SERVING: 200

Kluski na Parze, also known as pampuchy, are fluffy steamed dumplings that are a popular comfort food in Poland. They are often served with savory dishes like goulash or sweet toppings like fruit preserves and cream. These dumplings are a staple in many Polish households and are cherished for their light, airy texture.

Ingredients

You Need:

- 4 cups all-purpose flour
- 1 1/4 cups warm milk (110°F/45°C)
- 2 1/4 teaspoons (1 packet) active dry yeast
- 1/4 cup granulated sugar
- 2 large eggs
- 1/4 cup unsalted butter, melted
- 1 teaspoon salt
- 1 teaspoon vanilla extract (optional for sweet dumplings)

Directions

- **Prepare the Yeast Mixture:** In a small bowl, dissolve the yeast and a pinch of the sugar in the warm milk. Let it sit for about 10 minutes or until it becomes frothy.
- **Make the Dough:** In a large mixing bowl, combine the flour, remaining sugar, and salt. Add the yeast mixture, eggs, melted butter, and vanilla extract (if using) to the dry ingredients. Mix until the dough comes together, then knead for about 10 minutes until the dough is smooth and elastic. Knead the dough.
- **Let the Dough Rise:** Place the dough in a lightly oiled bowl, cover it with a clean kitchen towel, and let it rise in a warm place for about 45 minutes to 1 hour or until it has doubled in size.
- **Shape the Dumplings:** Once the dough has risen, punch it down and turn it out onto a floured surface. Divide the dough into 16 equal pieces and shape each piece into a smooth ball. Place the dough balls on a floured surface and let them rise for an additional 20 minutes.
- **Prepare the Steamer:** While the dumplings are rising, prepare a steamer. You can use a traditional steamer, a bamboo steamer, or a large pot with a steaming rack. Grease the steaming rack or line it with parchment paper to prevent sticking.
- **Steam the Dumplings:** Once the dumplings have risen, place them in the steamer, leaving enough space between them to allow for expansion. Cover the steamer and steam the dumplings over medium heat for about 10-12 minutes or until they are puffed up and cooked through. Do not lift the lid during the steaming process to ensure they cook evenly.

Kogel Mogel

PREP TIME: 5 MIN   **COOKING TIME: 5 MIN**   **SERVES: 1**   **CALORIES PER SERVING: 150**

Kogel Mogel is a traditional Polish dessert that dates back centuries. Its name comes from the Yiddish word "kugel" meaning "ball" or "round cake," and the German word "mogeln" meaning "to cheat" or "to trick." This dessert is often enjoyed as a sweet treat or used as a home remedy for sore throats.

Ingredients

You Need:
- 1 large egg
- 1 tablespoon honey or sugar
- 1 teaspoon unsalted butter
- Optional toppings: ground cinnamon, chopped nuts, cocoa powder, whipped cream

Directions

- **Prepare the Ingredients:** Crack the egg into a bowl, making sure not to break the yolk. Measure out the honey or sugar and set aside. Have any optional toppings ready for garnishing.

- **Mix the Ingredients:** In a small saucepan, melt the butter over low heat. Once the butter is melted, add the honey or sugar to the saucepan and stir until dissolved. Slowly pour the egg into the saucepan while continuously whisking to prevent the egg from scrambling. Cook the mixture over low heat, stirring constantly, until it thickens to a creamy consistency, similar to custard. This should take about 3-4 minutes. Be careful not to overcook, as the mixture can curdle.

Miodownik (Honey Cake)

PREP TIME: 30 MIN   **COOKING TIME: 30 MIN**   **SERVES: 12**   **CALORIES PER SERVING: 300**

Miodownik, or Polish Honey Cake, is a beloved dessert in Poland, especially during special occasions like birthdays and holidays. This cake is known for its rich flavor, moist texture, and aromatic spices. It's often enjoyed with a cup of tea or coffee, and its sweet aroma fills the kitchen as it bakes.

Ingredients

You Need:

Cake

- 2 cups all-purpose flour
- 1 teaspoon baking powder
- 1/2 teaspoon baking soda
- 1/2 teaspoon salt
- 1 teaspoon ground cinnamon
- 1/2 teaspoon ground cloves
- 1/2 teaspoon ground nutmeg
- 1/2 cup unsalted butter, softened
- 1/2 cup granulated sugar
- 3 large eggs
- 1 cup honey
- 1/2 cup sour cream
- 1 teaspoon vanilla extract

Frosting

- 1 1/2 cups heavy cream
- 1/4 cup powdered sugar
- 1 teaspoon vanilla extract

Directions

- **Preheat the Oven:** Preheat your oven to 350°F (175°C). Grease and flour a 9x13-inch baking pan.
- **Prepare the Dry Ingredients:** In a medium bowl, whisk together the flour, baking powder, baking soda, salt, cinnamon, cloves, and nutmeg until well combined. Set aside.
- **Make the Cake Batter:** In a large mixing bowl, cream together the softened butter and granulated sugar until light and fluffy. Add the eggs one at a time, beating well after each addition. Stir in the honey, sour cream, and vanilla extract until smooth. Gradually add the dry ingredients to the wet ingredients, mixing until just combined.
- **Bake the Cake:** Pour the cake batter into the prepared baking pan and spread it evenly. Bake in the preheated oven for 25-30 minutes or until a toothpick inserted into the center comes out clean. Remove the cake from the oven and let it cool completely in the pan on a wire rack.
- **Prepare the Frosting:** In a chilled mixing bowl, beat the heavy cream, powdered sugar, and vanilla extract until stiff peaks form.
- **Frost the Cake:** Once the cake has cooled completely, spread the whipped cream frosting evenly over the top. Optionally, sprinkle with additional ground cinnamon or chopped nuts for garnish.

Kutia (Fruit Wheat Berries)

PREP TIME: 9 HOUR   COOKING TIME: 1 HOUR   SERVES: 8   CALORIES PER SERVING: 250

Kutia is a traditional dish in Ukrainian, Polish, and Belarusian cuisine, often served during Christmas Eve dinner (Wigilia). It symbolizes prosperity, unity, and the cycle of life. Kutia is made with wheat berries, symbolizing hope and immortality, and is typically sweetened with honey and enriched with dried fruits and nuts.

Ingredients

You Need:
- 1 cup wheat berries
- 4 cups water (for soaking)
- 4 cups water (for cooking)
- 1/2 cup honey
- 1/2 cup chopped walnuts
- 1/4 cup raisins
- 1/4 cup dried cranberries or chopped dried apricots
- 1/4 teaspoon ground cinnamon
- 1/4 teaspoon ground cloves
- 1/4 teaspoon salt
- Optional toppings: chopped almonds, poppy seeds, additional honey

Directions

- **Soak the Wheat Berries:** Rinse the wheat berries under cold water. Place the wheat berries in a large bowl and cover them with 4 cups of water. Let the wheat berries soak for at least 8 hours or overnight.

- **Cook the Wheat Berries:** After soaking, drain the wheat berries and rinse them again under cold water. In a large pot, combine the soaked wheat berries with 4 cups of water. Bring the water to a boil over medium-high heat, then reduce the heat to low and simmer, covered, for about 1 hour, or until the wheat berries are tender but still chewy. Drain any excess water from the pot and transfer the cooked wheat berries to a large mixing bowl.

- **Prepare the Kutia:** To the cooked wheat berries, add the honey, chopped walnuts, raisins, dried cranberries or apricots, ground cinnamon, ground cloves, and salt. Stir well to combine all the ingredients.

Piernik (Polish Gingerbread)

PREP TIME: 20 MIN   COOKING TIME: 30 MIN   SERVES: 12   CALORIES PER SERVING: 250

Piernik, or Polish gingerbread, has a long and rich history in Polish cuisine. It dates back to the Middle Ages when spices like ginger, cinnamon, and cloves were highly prized and used sparingly in baking. Piernik is often associated with festive occasions, especially Christmas and Easter, and is traditionally decorated with intricate icing designs.

Ingredients

You Need:

Dry Ingredients
- 2 cups all-purpose flour
- 1 teaspoon baking soda
- 1 teaspoon ground cinnamon
- 1 teaspoon ground ginger
- 1/2 teaspoon ground cloves
- 1/4 teaspoon ground nutmeg
- 1/4 teaspoon salt

Wet Ingredients
- 1/2 cup unsalted butter, softened
- 1/2 cup granulated sugar
- 1/2 cup honey
- 1/4 cup milk
- 1 large egg

Optional Glaze:
- 1 cup powdered sugar
- 1-2 tablespoons milk
- 1/2 teaspoon vanilla extract

Directions

- **Preheat the Oven:** Preheat your oven to 350°F (175°C). Grease and flour a 9x9-inch baking pan.
- **Mix the Dry Ingredients:** In a medium bowl, whisk together the flour, baking soda, ground cinnamon, ground ginger, ground cloves, ground nutmeg, and salt until well combined. Set aside.
- **Cream the Butter and Sugar:** In a large mixing bowl, cream together the softened butter and granulated sugar until light and fluffy.
- **Add the Wet Ingredients:** Add the honey, milk, and egg to the creamed butter mixture. Beat until smooth and well combined.
- **Combine the Ingredients:** Gradually add the dry ingredients to the wet ingredients, mixing until a smooth dough forms.
- **Bake the Piernik:** Pour the dough into the prepared baking pan and spread it evenly. Bake in the preheated oven for 25-30 minutes, or until the top is firm to the touch and a toothpick inserted into the center comes out clean.
- **Cool and Glaze (Optional):** Allow the piernik to cool in the pan for 10 minutes, then transfer it to a wire rack to cool completely. If desired, prepare the glaze by whisking together the powdered sugar, milk, and vanilla extract until smooth. Drizzle the glaze over the cooled piernik.

Kluski Leniwe (Lazy Dumplings)

PREP TIME: 10 MIN   COOKING TIME: 15 MIN   SERVES: 4   CALORIES PER SERVING: 250

Kluski Leniwe, also known as "lazy dumplings" or "lazy noodles," is a traditional Polish dish that is quick and easy to make. It's called "lazy" because the dumplings are formed by simply dropping spoonfuls of dough into boiling water, without the need for shaping or rolling.

Ingredients

You Need:

- 2 cups farmer's cheese or dry cottage cheese
- 2 large eggs
- 1/4 cup granulated sugar
- 1/2 teaspoon vanilla extract
- 2 cups all-purpose flour
- Pinch of salt
- Butter or oil, for serving
- Optional toppings: sour cream, jam, cinnamon sugar

Directions

- **Prepare the Dough:** In a large mixing bowl, combine the farmer's cheese, eggs, granulated sugar, and vanilla extract. Mix until well combined. Add Flour and Salt: Gradually add the flour and a pinch of salt to the cheese mixture, stirring until a soft dough forms. The dough should be slightly sticky but manageable.

- **Boil Water:** Bring a large pot of salted water to a boil over medium-high heat.

- **Form the Dumplings:** Using a spoon, drop spoonfuls of the dough into the boiling water. The dumplings will puff up slightly as they cook, so don't overcrowd the pot.

- **Cook the Dumplings: Place the dumplings in boiling water for 3-4 minutes** or until they float to the surface and are cooked through.

- **Remove and Serve:** Use a slotted spoon to remove the cooked dumplings from the water and transfer them to a serving dish.

Kopernik (Copernicus Cake)

PREP TIME: 30 MIN   **COOKING TIME:** 30 MIN   **SERVES:** 12   **CALORIES PER SERVING:** 400

Kopernik, also known as Copernicus Cake, is a dessert named after the famous Polish astronomer Nicolaus Copernicus. This cake celebrates Copernicus's contributions to science and his Polish heritage.

Ingredients

You Need:

Sponge Cake Layers:

- 4 large eggs
- 1 cup granulated sugar
- 1 teaspoon vanilla extract
- 1 cup all-purpose flour
- 1 teaspoon baking powder
- Pinch of salt

Cream Filling:

- 2 cups heavy cream
- 1/4 cup powdered sugar
- 1 teaspoon vanilla extract

Chocolate Ganache:

- 1 cup semi-sweet chocolate chips
- 1/2 cup heavy cream

Directions

- **Prepare the Sponge Cake Layers:** Preheat your oven to 350°F (175°C). Grease and flour two 9-inch round cake pans. In a large mixing bowl, beat the eggs, granulated sugar, and vanilla extract until light and fluffy. In a separate bowl, sift together the flour, baking powder, and salt. Gradually add the dry ingredients to the egg mixture, mixing until well combined. Divide the batter evenly between the prepared cake pans and smooth the tops. Bake in the preheated oven for 25-30 minutes or until a toothpick inserted into the center comes out clean. Remove the cakes from the oven and let them cool in the pans for 10 minutes before transferring them to a wire rack to cool completely.
- **Prepare the Cream Filling:** In a chilled mixing bowl, whip the heavy cream, powdered sugar, and vanilla extract until stiff peaks form. Set aside.
- **Assemble the Cake:** Once the cake layers have cooled completely, place one layer on a serving plate or cake stand. Spread a generous layer of the whipped cream filling over the top of the cake layer. Place the second cake layer on top and press down gently to secure.
- **Make the Chocolate Ganache:** In a small saucepan, heat the heavy cream until it just begins to simmer. Remove the saucepan from the heat and add the chocolate chips. Let it sit for 1-2 minutes. Stir the mixture until the chocolate is completely melted and smooth.
- **Frost the Cake:** Pour the chocolate ganache over the top of the assembled cake, allowing it to drip down the sides. Use a spatula to spread the ganache evenly over the top and sides of the cake.
- **Chill the Cake:** Place the cake in the refrigerator to chill for at least 2 hours or until the ganache is set.

Krówki (Polish Milk Fudge)

PREP TIME: 5 MIN   **COOKING TIME: 20 MIN**   **SERVES: 24**   **CALORIES PER SERVING: 80**

Krówki, which translates to "little cows" in Polish, are traditional Polish milk fudge candies that have been enjoyed for generations. They are named for their resemblance to small cow-shaped candies. Krowki are known for their creamy texture and rich, caramelized flavor, making them a beloved treat in Poland and beyond.

Ingredients

You Need:
- 1 cup granulated sugar
- 1 cup heavy cream
- 2 tablespoons unsalted butter
- 1 teaspoon vanilla extract
- Pinch of salt
- Confectioners' sugar, for dusting (optional)

Directions

- **Prepare the Pan:** Line an 8x8-inch baking dish with parchment paper, leaving an overhang on two sides. This will make it easier to lift the fudge out of the pan later.
- **Cook the Fudge:** In a medium saucepan, combine the granulated sugar, heavy cream, unsalted butter, vanilla extract, and a pinch of salt. Cook the mixture over medium heat, stirring constantly, until the sugar has dissolved and the mixture comes to a boil.
- **Simmer:** Reduce the heat to medium-low and continue to cook the mixture, stirring frequently, until it reaches the soft-ball stage (about 238°F/114°C on a candy thermometer). This should take about 15-20 minutes.
- **Cool the Mixture:** Once the mixture reaches the soft-ball stage, immediately remove it from the heat and pour it into the prepared baking dish.
- **Shape the Fudge:** Let the fudge cool in the baking dish for a few minutes until it is cool enough to handle but still pliable. Using a buttered knife or bench scraper, cut the fudge into small squares while it is still warm.
- **Let it Set:** Allow the fudge squares to cool completely at room temperature for about 1 hour or until firm.

Faworki (Angel Wings)

PREP TIME: 30 MIN   COOKING TIME: 20 MIN   SERVES: 24   CALORIES PER SERVING: 100

Faworki, also known as "Angel Wings," are a traditional Polish pastry enjoyed during special occasions like Fat Thursday (Tłusty Czwartek) and other festive celebrations. These delicate, deep-fried pastries are named for their intricate, wing-like shape, resembling angel wings.

Ingredients

You Need:

- 2 cups all-purpose flour
- 2 tablespoons granulated sugar
- 2 large eggs
- 2 tablespoons sour cream
- 2 tablespoons unsalted butter, melted
- 1/4 teaspoon salt
- 1 teaspoon vanilla extract
- Vegetable oil, for frying
- Powdered sugar, for dusting

Directions

- **Prepare the Dough:** In a large mixing bowl, combine the flour, granulated sugar, and salt. In a separate bowl, beat the eggs, then add the sour cream, melted butter, and vanilla extract. Mix until well combined. Gradually add the wet ingredients to the dry ingredients, stirring until a smooth dough forms. If the dough is too sticky, you can add a little more flour.
- **Roll out the Dough:** On a lightly floured surface, roll out the dough to about 1/8 inch thickness. Use a rolling pin to achieve an even thickness.
- **Cut into Strips:** Using a sharp knife or a pastry cutter cut the rolled-out dough into strips that are about 1 inch wide and 4-5 inches long.
- **Form the Angel Wings:** Make a small slit in the center of each strip of dough. Pull one end of the strip through the slit to form a twisted loop resembling angel wings. Repeat with the remaining strips of dough.
- **Heat the Oil:** In a large, deep saucepan or fryer, heat vegetable oil to 350°F (175°C) over medium heat. You'll need enough oil to completely submerge the angel wings.
- **Fry the Angel Wings:** Carefully place a few angel wings into the hot oil, being careful not to overcrowd the pan. Fry them in batches if necessary. Fry the angel wings for about 2-3 minutes on each side or until they are golden brown and crispy.
- **Drain and Cool:** Use a slotted spoon to remove the fried angel wings from the oil and transfer them to a paper towel-lined plate to drain excess oil. Allow the angel wings to cool completely before dusting them with powdered sugar.

Kokosanki (Coconut Balls)

PREP TIME: 15 MIN   **COOKING TIME: NONE**   **SERVES: 20**   **CALORIES PER SERVING: 120**

Kokosanki, or Coconut Balls, are a popular Polish sweet treat enjoyed during holidays and special occasions. These delightful confections are made with simple ingredients like coconut, condensed milk, and butter, and are often flavored with vanilla or rum extract.

Ingredients

You Need:

- 2 cups sweetened shredded coconut
- 1/2 cup sweetened condensed milk
- 2 tablespoons unsalted butter, melted
- 1/2 teaspoon vanilla extract
- Pinch of salt
- Additional shredded coconut, for coating (optional)

Directions

- **Prepare the Mixture:** In a large mixing bowl, combine the sweetened shredded coconut, sweetened condensed milk, melted unsalted butter, vanilla extract, and a pinch of salt. Stir the ingredients together until well combined and the mixture holds together when pressed.

- **Shape the Coconut Balls:** Take small portions of the coconut mixture and roll them between your palms to form balls about 1 inch in diameter. If desired, roll the coconut balls in additional shredded coconut for an extra coating.

- **Chill the Coconut Balls:** Place the formed coconut balls on a baking sheet lined with parchment paper. Transfer the baking sheet to the refrigerator and chill the coconut balls for at least 1 hour or until they are firm.

Sękacz (Polish Tree Cake)

PREP TIME: 30 MIN   COOKING TIME: 1 HOUR   SERVES: 8-9   CALORIES PER SERVING: 300

Sękacz, also known as "Polish Tree Cake" or "Tree Cake," is a traditional Polish dessert that originated in the Mazovia region. This unique cake is made by pouring thin layers of batter onto a rotating spit or wooden pole over an open fire or special oven. As each layer cooks, it forms a ring, creating the appearance of tree rings.

Ingredients

You Need:

- 8 large eggs
- 1 cup granulated sugar
- 1 cup all-purpose flour
- 1 teaspoon vanilla extract
- 1/2 teaspoon almond extract (optional)
- 1/2 cup unsalted butter, melted
- Powdered sugar, for dusting

Directions

- **Preheat the Oven:** Preheat your oven to 350°F (175°C). Grease and flour a sękacz mold or bundt cake pan.
- **Prepare the Batter:** In a large mixing bowl, beat the eggs and granulated sugar together until pale and fluffy. Add the vanilla extract and almond extract (if using) to the egg mixture and mix until combined. Gradually add the flour to the egg mixture, stirring until smooth. Slowly pour in the melted unsalted butter and mix until well combined.
- **Bake the Cake:** Pour a thin layer of batter into the prepared sękacz mold or bundt cake pan, spreading it evenly. Place the mold or pan in the preheated oven and bake for about 5-7 minutes, or until the layer is set and lightly golden brown. Remove the mold or pan from the oven and pour another thin layer of batter on top of the first layer. Repeat this process until all the batter is used, alternating layers until the mold or pan is filled.
- **Bake Until Done:** Continue baking the sękacz for about 1 hour, or until a toothpick inserted into the center comes out clean and the cake is golden brown. If the top of the cake starts to brown too quickly, cover it loosely with aluminum foil to prevent burning.
- **Cool and Serve:** Once baked, remove the sękacz from the oven and let it cool in the mold or pan for 10-15 minutes. Carefully invert the cake onto a wire rack and allow it to cool completely. Once cooled, dust the sękacz with powdered sugar for decoration.

Wuzetki (Polish Chocolate Cream Cake)

PREP TIME: 30 MIN   **COOKING TIME:** 25 MIN   **SERVES:** 12   **CALORIES PER SERVING:** 400

Wuzetki, also known as "Polish Chocolate Cream Cake," is a decadent dessert that combines layers of rich chocolate cake with creamy chocolate frosting. This indulgent cake is a favorite among chocolate lovers in Poland and is often served during special occasions and celebrations.

Ingredients
You Need:

For the Chocolate Cake Layers
- 1 and 3/4 cups all-purpose flour
- 1 and 1/2 cups granulated sugar
- 3/4 cup unsweetened cocoa powder
- 1 and 1/2 teaspoons baking powder
- 1 and 1/2 teaspoons baking soda
- 1 teaspoon salt
- 2 large eggs
- 1 cup buttermilk
- 1/2 cup vegetable oil
- 2 teaspoons vanilla extract
- 1 cup hot water

For the Chocolate Cream Frosting
- 1 cup unsalted butter, softened
- 3 and 1/2 cups powdered sugar
- 1/2 cup unsweetened cocoa powder
- 1/4 cup heavy cream
- 1 teaspoon vanilla extract
- Pinch of salt

Directions

- **Prepare the Chocolate Cake Layers:** Preheat your oven to 350°F (175°C). Grease and flour two 9-inch round cake pans. In a large mixing bowl, sift together the flour, granulated sugar, cocoa powder, baking powder, baking soda, and salt. Add the eggs, buttermilk, vegetable oil, and vanilla extract to the dry ingredients. Mix until well combined. Gradually pour in the hot water and mix until the batter is smooth. Divide the batter evenly between the prepared cake pans. Bake in the preheated oven for 25-30 minutes or until a toothpick inserted into the center of the cakes comes out clean. Remove the cakes from the oven and let them cool in the pans for 10 minutes before transferring them to a wire rack to cool completely.

- **Make the Chocolate Cream Frosting:** In a large mixing bowl, beat the softened butter until creamy. Gradually add the powdered sugar and cocoa powder to the butter, mixing until smooth and well combined. Add the heavy cream, vanilla extract, and pinch of salt to the frosting, and beat until light and fluffy.

- **Assemble the Cake:** Once the cake layers have cooled completely, place one layer on a serving plate or cake stand. Spread a thick layer of chocolate cream frosting over the top of the first cake layer. Place the second cake layer on top and press down gently to secure. Use the remaining chocolate cream frosting to frost the top and sides of the cake.

- **Chill the Cake:** Place the assembled cake in the refrigerator to chill for at least 2 hours or until the frosting is set.

Conclusion

In the heart of every Polish family lies a treasure trove of culinary traditions, passed down through generations like cherished heirlooms. As we conclude our journey through the pages of this cookbook, we find ourselves not only satiated by the flavors and aromas of Poland but also enriched by the stories and memories woven into each recipe.

We have embarked on a culinary odyssey that transcends mere ingredients and techniques. We have delved into the very essence of Polish culture, where food is not merely sustenance but a language of love, connection, and heritage. From the bustling markets of Krakow to the quaint kitchens of rural villages, each recipe tells a story—a story of resilience, of community, and of the enduring bonds of family.

Yet, even as we celebrate tradition, we also embrace innovation. Polish cuisine is a living, breathing entity, constantly evolving to reflect the changing tastes and influences of the modern world. In the kitchens of Poland, ancient recipes mingle with contemporary ingredients, resulting in a vibrant tapestry of flavors that speak to the country's dynamic culinary landscape.

In closing, we extend our heartfelt gratitude to the countless individuals who have contributed to this cookbook. To the grandmothers who have lovingly shared their secret recipes, to the chefs who have painstakingly preserved the traditions of the past, and to the families who have opened their homes and hearts to us, we say **dziękuję**. It is through your generosity, your passion, and your unwavering commitment to preserving Poland's culinary heritage that this cookbook has come to life.

And so, as we embark on our own culinary adventures, let us carry with us the spirit of Poland—the spirit of tradition, of innovation, and above all, of togetherness. For in the end, it is not the dishes we cook but the memories we create, the stories we share, and the love we nourish that truly define the essence of Polish cuisine.

Wishing you many happy hours spent in the kitchen, savoring the flavors of Poland and creating memories that will last a lifetime.

Smacznego!

Babcia Wera

Chapter Six

Glossary

First Courses

1. Pierogi - "Pye-roh-ghee"

2. Gołąbki - "Go-wump-kee"

3. Kotlet Schabowy - "Kot-let Sha-boh-vih"

4. Kiełbasa z Kapustą - "Kyehw-bah-sah z Kah-poo-stah"

5. Kopytka - "Koh-pit-kah"

6. Placki Ziemniaczane - "Plat-skee Zhyem-nya-chah-neh"

7. Śledź w Śmietanie - "Swedj v Shmye-tah-neh"

8. Zrazy - "Zrah-zi"

9. Pierś z Kurczak - "Pyersh z Kur-chak"

10. Kaszanka - "Kah-shahn-kah"

11. Flaki - "Flah-kee"

12. Kluski Śląskie - "Kloo-skee Swon-skyeh"

13. Kotlety Mielone - "Kot-let-ee Myeh-loh-neh"

14. Żurek - "Zhoo-rek"

15. Kluski z Makiem - "Kloo-skee z Mah-kyem"

16. Golonka - "Goh-lon-kah"

17. Krokiety - "Kroh-kyeh-tee"

18. Kapusta Zasmażana - "Kah-poos-tah Zah-smah-zha-nah"

19. Kopytka ze Śmietaną - "Koh-pit-kah zeh Shmye-tah-nah"

20. Kapusta Zasmażana z Kiełbasą - "Kah-poos-tah Zah-smah-zha-nah z Kyehw-bah-sah"

21. Krokiety z Mięsem - "Kroh-kyeh-tee z Myen-sem"

22. Zupa Pomidorowa - "Zoo-pah Poh-mee-doh-roh-vah"

23. Jajka w Sosie Tatarskim - "Yahy-kah v Soh-shyeh Tah-tar-skeem"

24. Ryba po Grecku - "Rih-bah poh Greh-tsoo"

25. Kulebiak - "Koo-leb-yahk"

Soups

1. Barszcz - "Barshch"

2. Żurek - "Zhoo-rek"

3. Kapusniak - "Kah-poosh-nyahk"

4. Rosół - "Roh-soow"

5. Zupa Grzybowa - "Zoo-pah Gzhib-oh-vah"

6. Chłodnik - "Hwoo-dneek"

7. Krupnik - "Kroop-neek"

8. Zupa Pomidorowa - "Zoo-pah Poh-mee-doh-roh-vah"

9. Kapusta Kiszoną - "Kah-poos-tah Kee-shoh-naw"

10. Śledź w Śmietanie - "Swedj v Shmye-tah-neh"

11. Flaki - "Flah-kee"

12. Grochówka - "Groh-hoov-kah"

13. Kapusniak z Grochem - "Kah-poosh-nyahk z Groh-hem"

14. Zupa Fasolowa - "Zoo-pah Fah-soh-loh-vah"

15. Kluski z Rosołu - "Kloo-skee z Roh-soow"

Appetizers

1. Pasztet - "Pahsh-tet"

2. Śledź w Oleju - "Shledj v Oh-lye-oo"

3. Kiełbasa - "Kyehw-bah-sah"

4. Sałatka Jarzynowa - "Sah-wat-kah Yah-zhi-noh-vah"

5. Kulebiak - "Koo-leb-yahk"

6. Placki Ziemniaczane - "Plat-skee Zhyem-nya-chah-neh"

7. Rolady - "Roh-lah-dih"

8. Naleśniki - "Nah-lesh-nee-kee"

9. Pasztet drobiowy - "Pahsh-tet droh-byoh-vih"

10. Gołąbki - "Go-wump-kee"

11. Jajka Faszerowane - "Yahy-kah Fah-sheh-roh-vah-neh"

12. Paszteciki - "Pahsh-teh-chee-kee"

13. Placki Drożdżowe - "Plat-skee Droh-zhdoh-veh"

14. Kotlety Mielone - "Kot-let-ee Myeh-loh-neh"

15. Jajka w Majonezie - "Yahy-kah v Mah-yoh-neh-zeh"

16. Półmisek Zakąsek - "Poow-mee-sek Zah-kon-sek"

17. Pomidory Faszerowane - "Poh-mee-doh-ri Fah-sheh-roh-vah-neh"

18. Kaszanka na Ciepło - "Kah-shahn-kah nah Chyeh-pwoh"

19. Kanapki - "Kah-nahp-kee"

20. Pierogi z Serem - "Pyeh-roh-gee z Seh-rem"

Drinks

1. Kompot - "Kohm-pot")

2. Cytrynówka - "Tsih-trih-noov-kah"

3. Krówka - "Kroov-kah"

4. Miód pitny - "Myoot peet-nih"

5. Piwo z miodem - "Pee-voh z myoh-dem"

6. Herbata z Prątnic - "Her-bah-tah z Prohnt-neets"

7. Oranżada - "Oh-rahn-zhah-dah"

8. Kwas Chlebowy - "Kvahs Hleh-boh-vih"

9. Sirop Malinowy - "See-rohp Mah-lee-noh-vih"

10. Zsiadłe Mleko - "Zshyah-dweh Mleh-koh"

Desserts

1. Paczki - "Pohnch-kee"

2. Sernik - "Ser-neek"

3. Makowiec - "Mah-koh-vyets"

4. Naleśniki - "Nah-lesh-nee-kee"

5. Szarlotka - "Shar-lot-kah"

6. Kremówka - "Kreh-moov-kah"

7. Pączki z Marmoladą - "Pohnch-kee z Mar-moh-lah-doh"

8. Ptasie Mleczko - "Ptah-syeh Mlehch-koh"

9. Kluski Śląskie - "Kloo-skee Swon-skyeh"

10. Kluski na Parze - "Kloo-skee nah Pah-zeh"

11. Kogel Mogel - "Koh-gel Moh-gel"

12. Miodownik - "Myoh-dohv-neek"

13. Kutia - "Koo-tyah"

14. Piernik - "Pyehr-neek"

15. Kluski Leniwe - "Kloo-skee Leh-nee-veh"

16. Kopernik - "Koh-pehr-neek"

17. Krowki - "Kroof-kee"

18. Faworki - "Fah-vor-kee"

19. Kokosanki - "Koh-koh-sahn-kee"

20. Sękacz - "Sen-kach"

21. Wuzetki - "Voo-zet-kee"

www.ingramcontent.com/pod-product-compliance
Lightning Source LLC
Chambersburg PA
CBHW082211070526

44585CB00020B/2367